Praise for

Reading *The Soul Watchers* reminded me that opening our minds to the incredible value animals have in our world can be very awakening and healing at the same time. Kim provides a unique perspective on the role animals play in our lives if we seek their wisdom and true companionship. She adeptly teaches readers how to bring animals' knowledge into their consciousness and use it to improve their own life experience.

— MICHELLE MANTOR, PUBLISHER AND EDITOR-IN-CHIEF
OF *HOUSTON PETTALK AND PETTALKGOFETCH*

Few things in life are more precious than the bond we share with our beloved pets. *The Soul Watchers* is an enjoyable read for everyone who knows the love of a pet and wants to explore the blessings of the living world around us. My favorite parts of the book are the spiritual parts, as well as the quotes at the beginning of each chapter. As someone who deals with sickness and loss regularly, it is reassuring that all things happen for a reason, and that there are plenty of other forces at work in this world that are beyond our control. This gives me the perspective that we humans are a piece of the whole. We work with nature, and nature wants to partner with us. I plan to go back through the action steps as anchors for getting more out of my second reading.

— JESSICA PARKERSON, DVM

Kim really delivers in this book. It's the ultimate reference guide to all things holistic for animal care. I'll be using it often. It also invites us (with directions) to connect to our inner wisdom, expand our hearts and be more of our best selves in our interactions with animals—from our past, our present, and even our future. The action steps in each chapter offer a huge payoff.

— HELEN RACZ, EFT PRACTITIONER, LIFE COACH, AUTHOR OF
TELL ME WHERE YOU'RE STUCK AND *THE LOGICAL LAW OF ATTRACTION*

Praise for *The Soul Watchers*

I loved this book! It opened up my mind and soul to new things that I wasn't aware of. I never realized how many tools we have within to help us understand and communicate with animals. I can see myself reading this multiple times and learning new things from it every time. Parts of it brought me back into a space where I really need to be— for myself, for my animals, and for humanity!

— DAWN SACRE, PET PARENT

This book belongs on every animal lover's reading list! It contains groundbreaking information on the physical, mental, emotional, and spiritual life of animals, including how to use many unique healing modalities. There's a wealth of information here that newcomers and even the most experienced animal communicators can learn from. I certainly did!

— LINDA CLAYTON, AUTHOR OF *LOOK WHO'S TALKING*, *A PERSONAL JOURNEY INTO ANIMAL COMMUNICATION*

The Soul Watchers is a must-have book for anyone seeking a more meaningful and deeper connection with the animals in their lives. Kim shows how we can open ourselves to the wisdom of Mother Nature and the animal kingdom, empowering us to make this world a more loving and enlightened place. You will see all animals as kindred spirits. Once I started reading, I couldn't put it down! I love the action steps. Each time I do one of these steps, I get new meaning and new messages.

— MICHELLE PORLIER, PET PARENT, VETERINARY RECEPTIONIST, KINDRED SPIRIT TO THE ANIMALS

Kim is a clear intuitive of truth, wisdom, and love for all our animals and nature Spirits. Her passion and gift for our light world is to teach us to open our hearts and allow the animals to assist us in raising our vibration to a place where we can heal and discover our true essence.

— LAURIE NERI BARRETT, HUMAN AND ANIMAL WELLNESS COACH, AUTHOR OF *PRACTICAL WELLNESS*

Praise for *The Soul Watchers*

Kim's lifelong love for and dedication to animals is an inspiration to us all. Her first book, *The Soul Watchers,* is groundbreaking in that we discover the communication with our beloved pets—even with animals in the wild—is not a one-way street. Kim shows us how they share this planet with us for the welfare of our souls. The book is full of fascinating stories and photos from her many experiences. In addition, Kim shares her expertise in the many aspects of holistic animal care, which opens up a new world of choices for us to improve the quality of our pets' lives.

— DENIS OUELLETTE, SEMINAR LEADER, AUTHOR OF
HEAL YOURSELF WITH BREATH, LIGHT, SOUND & WATER

I have been blessed to learn holistic animal care, as shared in *The Soul Watchers,* directly from Kim and Allison (The Lightfoot Way). You are now blessed to personally learn how much animals have to teach us. As a pet-care professional, I've learned that when we are open to possibilities, we will never cease to be amazed at what our animal friends want to share and teach us. So much joy, light and peace has come to me since I opened myself to learning more about holistic care and the wonder of animals and nature. I hope you too will enjoy your deeper journey with animals.

— SUSAN BRIGGS, CPACO, CO-FOUNDER OF THE DOG GURUS,
CO-AUTHOR OF *OFF-LEASH DOG PLAY*

Upon reading this sacred learning journey with animals, I am validated in my own knowing that all animals have a higher purpose, which includes us. How lucky are we to have such unconditionally loving companions in our lives who sometimes can do for us what another human cannot. I find that miraculous. Kim's profound teachings will bring great comfort and consciousness expansion to those called to work with animals and their owners. What a blessing that this knowledge has come into the world through Kim, and through the animals she has served and who have served her.

— LINDA M. GALVAN, MA, SPIRITUAL INTUITIVE SOUL GUIDE, PURE LIGHT
CHANNEL, SACRED ALCHEMIST, TRANSFORMATIONAL FACILITATOR

Praise for *The Soul Watchers*

The Soul Watchers takes the entire spectrum of natural healing, plants and animal communication and breaks it down into a basic, easy to digest manner where anyone can pick up this book and feel so empowered. Kim takes the intimidation out of all these subjects and makes it so easy to understand while sharing their ancient origins. Why have we as a society made things so difficult and complex instead of an easy flowing, almost effortless understanding of all these ancient truths. I love her simple but powerful intention in regards to talking to animals.

—CINDIE CARTER, HOST OF THE SOCIAL DOG PODCAST

Beautifully shared stories, insights and guidance for the Heart. Practice even just a few of Kim's many valuable suggestions filling this book and you will open yourself to a deeper level of listening with animals, nature and even yourself!

—MEGAN AYRAULT, LMT, ZERO BALANCING PRACTITIONER, FOUNDER OF POWER OF TOUCH FOR ANIMALS

If you have ever been curious about why you feel connected or drawn to certain animals or items in nature, *The Soul Watchers* will be your guide to start on a journey that may forever change your life. This book provides action steps to help you better connect with yourself, nature and all types of animals. Kim has spent years on her journey to discovering the teachings provided by animals and nature that most of us miss due to not being able to recognize what we are seeing. In this book she shares what she has learned and poses questions for you to answer along your own journey.

—JESSICA MARZIANI, DVM, CVA, CVC, CCRT

Praise for *The Soul Watchers*

I just finished reading Kim Shotola's new book, *The Soul Watchers, Animals' Quest to Awaken Humanity*. From some reason, I had been putting this off and making excuses on how busy I was and had several other stressful events going on to deal with, so was feeling negative and somewhat depressed. I finally sat down and started to read this book, it was exactly what I needed at this time.

This book affirmed a lot of my beliefs and reminded me of the positive nature of animals and healing spirit of nature and animals. I believe that things happen for a reason and I have devoted my life to helping animals, so I should have known to sit down and start reading this sooner! I love the quotes at the beginning of each chapter. Kim sets a clear path on how we can help our animals and how they help us heal and enrich our lives. This is a must read for all animal lovers!

—Robin Robinett, DVM, CVC, CVA,
Veterinary Chiropractic and Rehabilitation Clinic

As guardians, we are tasked with continual learning and growing as a part of our journey with animals, with the goal of becoming the best caretakers and stewards we can possibly become. At some point in our personal evolution we inevitably end up with questions about energy and energy transfer. Sometimes healthcare professionals are asked about the non-physical aspects of animals: about omens and signs from the Natural World and how to interpret them.

Of course, not everyone is interested in metaphysical connections or meanings, but if your interest is piqued, the next question is often "where can I learn more?" Thankfully, there are an infinite number of paths, processes and resources, including this book, that offer insights that may resonate with you. The goal is to search until you find answers that align with your core, provide a deep sense of peace, and ultimately allow you to become the best, most evolved version of yourself. This is when fear dissipates and you become keenly aware of your eternal and ongoing connection with all living things.

—Karen Becker, DVM

*Greetings and may the Peace of God be with you
as you read the wisdom that my beloved Kim has prepared for you.
She has come to the garden of Earth at this time to bring the wisdom
of the ages of how God created the fraternal existence between
all creatures of the Earth. This beloved soul imparts joy eternal
in her demonstrating realignment into full health, love, and peaceful
existence for all inhabitants of God's beautiful Earth. Her teachings
are the Truth, for even the smallest sparrow is precious in the sight
of God. Allow her words and love to awaken your heart
and broaden your awareness to know that ALL ARE ONE.
I bless this work and publication, and I bless you.*

—Your brother, Francis (Giovanni) di Assisi,
channeled through Jana Lynne (Nov. 12, 2019)

The Soul Watchers

Animals' Quest to Awaken Humanity

Kim Shotola

the
LIGHTFOOT
WAY

The Soul Watchers
Animals' Quest to Awaken Humanity

Kim Shotola

Print ISBN: 978-1-7332012-4-7

Printed in the United States of America

Cover design and layout by Denis Ouellette
Edited by Linda Locke

The Lightfoot Way
7 Paradise Ranch Road
Livingston, Montana 59047

For additional copies, visit:
TheLightfootWay.com
Amazon.com

Dedication

*Bless the souls of the animals,
for they have been faithfully watching
over ours.*

CONTENTS

CONTENTS

ACKNOWLEDGMENTS

One of my students, a talented Irish author,
lovingly dedicated one of his books in his trilogy to me.
I wondered when I wrote my first book, who all I would recognize.

Scott, you've been an amazing husband,
believer and supporter in everything I do.

Karalee, my wonderful daughter,
I'm so proud of the kindred spirit you have become.

My beautiful Mom, my friend, who imparted to me
a lifelong love for animals and plants.

Karl, you're a great brother
who makes me laugh and spurs on my dreams.

Nana, my grandmother, whose soul still watches over me
and cheers my passion on.

Allison, my business partner and soul sister,
I wouldn't be where I am without you.

Susan, you shine a path for professionals to know animals
on a heart and soul level.

Laurie, your incredible strength lies not only in helping people,
but also helping animals.

Thank you to our incredible students, Cassandra, Joel, Michelle
and Natalie, for the inspirational words of wisdom from my animals.

ACKNOWLEDGMENTS

To our dedicated students from all over the world,
you are why we do this.

Dr. Marcia DuBois Martin, thank you for my professional start
at your animal clinic.

Dr. Jessica Marziani, my personal animals and the zoo animals
are forever grateful.

To all my fellow zooper zoo friends,
you're an integral part of my life and in my heart.

Thanks to Denis, my brilliant book advisor and designer,
and Linda, my eagle-eyed editor.

To my special heart and soul animals,
Diamond, Rain and Tara.

I'm grateful for all of the animals that have touched my life,
and for those that will.

To all of the animals and people we have had the honor of helping.
You know who you are. It started with a yellow lab named Marlie
and grew from there. Cindy, we thank you for sharing Marlie with us
and becoming a special friend.

And Fergus, you've inspired me with your poetic, literary diversity.
Perhaps there's a trilogy in me.

Introduction

Animals have been watching your soul since before you were born. Their quest is to oversee our souls' journey and to awaken and enlighten our hearts and souls to the connection between them, nature and Mother Earth. Animals are here to help each person become better on a heart and soul level.

Our pets can bring us joy, companionship, strength, love and comfort. But their efforts go far beyond that. You may have animals in your life right now, or you did at one time. Or perhaps you just love animals and have not taken on that pet parent or foster role yet. Perhaps you are going through a difficult time in your life or feel lost. Maybe you just *know* or *feel* there has got to be more to life than this. The animals can show you the present, help you learn from the past, and propel you to your future.

There are more animals trying to "reach" you than you may realize—even right now. You have a divine purpose, and yes, the animals play an instrumental role in helping you discover AND accomplish this. The animals can show you how to awaken your life physically, mentally, emotionally and spiritually. Just like they did for me.

I have always loved animals since I was a child. They have always been a constant in my life, and in ways I only discovered later, watched over me. When my parents went through an ugly divorce when my brother and I were just 6 and 7, the animals were there. When my father died tragically just several years later, the animals were there.

At 12 years old, I waited on customers at my mom's plant nursery on the weekends. Our nursery was not just for plants. We helped raise several species of pet birds, which brought us joy and additional income. At 14, I bred, raised and sold championship pedigreed collies. Little did I know that collies were to become a major part of my life for over 30 years. Go Lassie!

The cats and other dogs that I shared my life with were amazing rescues. All kinds of pets have blessed my life from gerbils, hamsters, guinea pigs and chinchillas to hermit crabs, turtles, rabbits, parakeets, cockatiels, conures, doves, ducks, turkeys, guinea fowl, chickens, cows and horses. And how could I forget tadpoles, frogs and toads.

Some animals found me. Some I found. I have loved them all.

The animals guided me to a career with them. From 1991–2017, I worked full-time at the Houston Zoo in Texas, a world-class and renowned zoo recognized for their exceptional animal care and global conservation efforts. I progressed from zookeeper to senior supervisor during my 25+ year career. I helped manage the care of over 1,000 domestic, livestock, wildlife and exotic animals in the Children's Zoo, including the animal ambassadors that were used in public presentations. I even supervised the staff of the incredible bug house. But the above figure doesn't count the thousands of creatures that resided there—and when they have babies—it's a lot! A highlight for me was when I taught and educated staff, volunteers and guests about the magnificent world of animals, big and small. I was even featured on a number of local TV stations, including in the NBC affiliate series, *Houston Zooperstars Challenge,* that ran for several years.

But while I was working at the zoo, I also reflected inward. Perhaps it was only natural for me to explore ways to help heal my body, mind, and spirit. I was wounded on various levels. Between my parents' divorce and my father's death, you could say a "nightmare" ensued for my brother and I. That led to stomach and OCD issues.

I realized my childhood and animals had brought me to this point of seeking a path to wellness and wholeness. From nutrition to energy work to animal communication and more, I was hooked for life! But what blew me away was the realization that what I had learned over the years for myself, I could also use to help animals! Through the process of helping my own animals, I knew they wanted me to do more to help the lives of other animals and those who cared for them.

And so it began. I was then led to reach and teach animal lovers from all over the world how to help strengthen their connection, prevent illness, and heal the animals in their care. In 2006, I started my animal wellness practice. I offered consultations and taught classes in the evenings and on weekends. The following year, my business partner Allison, who has become my best friend and soul sister, joined my journey. The Lightfoot Way was born.

The name has special significance to me. I have been drawn to the Native American culture since I was young. My homes have always reflected this. I feel everyone should tread lightly on Mother Earth and have respect for all creatures and life. When we give to others, we are truly blessed.

I have loved sharing the knowledge the animals have given me to empower others. I have cherished seeing animals and people live happier, healthier and longer lives. And one of my greatest joys was bringing holistic care to the zoo.

I saw the animals receive acupuncture, chiropractic and laser therapy from my personal vets, and aromatherapy and massage from the trained zookeepers. So many zoo animals have benefited from this heart and soul care, such as goats, pigs and deer to coatis, big cats, sea turtles, and even komodo dragons. Who knew that what I started at the Houston Zoo years ago would eventually evolve into the opportunity for other zoos to become awakened.

Animals have guided me. I am here because of them. My life would not be the same without them. If you think about your pets, you probably feel the same way, too. I feel their wisdom has helped me to become a beacon of light for them and others. If you let the animals help you on your path, you too, will become a shining beacon of radiant light. And together, we are a brilliant and magnified ray of hope for the animals and the world. Together, we help the animals fulfill their ultimate mission.

I wrote this book to share the knowledge I have gained. I hope it will teach you the depths of the Soul Watchers' mission and how to put it into action on a heart and soul level. It will even teach you about your own care and help you to be a better person amongst humanity. Interestingly, when I went to write the title of the book, I started to spell *Humanity* with *You*. I then wrote it out "You-manity." You see, YOU are an integral part of this greater picture. One person can help influence another, and so on. This is the Soul Watcher effect.

Animals are a window to your soul and a doorway to your spiritual destiny. If you let them into your life and allow the soul watchers to teach you, you will awaken your heart and soul like never before. By reading this book, I feel you will never look at animals or nature the same way again. I truly believe you will also look at yourself differently—your eyes will be opened, and your life will forever be changed. Together, we can accomplish the mission the animals have for us, to awaken humanity's consciousness for the benefit of all life on Mother Earth.

Remember to go to www.TheSoulWatchers.com to sign up to get access to your complementary follow-along guide and audio meditation!

Heart & Soul Blessings!

Kim

GUIDE NOTES: *Take your time to complete the guide. It may take you days to get through it or a month or more. This is an exercise of the heart and soul. There is no time-line, so take your time.*

Prologue

Rain was a wolf dog I was blessed to have come into my life for four short years. My partner, Allison, forwarded an email to me that had been circulated. Rain needed a home by Christmas Eve or would be euthanized. Immediately when I saw her photo, I felt a connection so strong and knew I was supposed to give her that home. In return, she gave me so much more, beyond my wildest dreams. She wanted very much to be a part of this book. It was her honor to share her soul with you, in hopes that her words would touch and impact the deepest part of your soul:

Who are you? You are a being of light. You may not realize it, as perhaps you feel any light in you has been snuffed out. Or maybe you feel a tiny flicker. Or maybe a radiant glow streams forth. However you find the state of your inner flame to be, please know that it has the capacity to get even brighter. As you start this journey, keep an open mind and an open heart. There will be things you are already aware of and other things that will take you by surprise. Be willing to step outside of your box, one foot at a time. You are here because you are meant to be here. You are reading this by no accident. Your soul is ready to encounter and expand like never before.

Sometimes, we do not realize how we can be a ray of hope for others. You are that ray of hope for us, for all creatures and mankind. For without you, the world would be a different place. You are an important piece of this global puzzle that we try to construct for peace. Please know that you never walk this road alone. The animals will always be there for you. I will be there for you. Use the knowledge you glean from this book to make a difference. Turn that spark into a glorious fire and let it ignite the world. A world we all need to understand on a heart and soul level—as one. May our light strengthen your light and empower you on this sacred path.

With All My Soul,
Rain

Chapter 1

The Soul Watchers' Quest

Be curious and never stop learning.
Be curious about all of the animals in the world,
because they all have something they can teach you.
Let your curiosity lead the way.

—BANDIT, MY DOG IN SPIRIT

To some, a quest might sound like some romanticized adventure in Sherwood Forest, a magical kingdom or perhaps a journey with Indiana Jones. Well, to all of the animals, this quest is real and has been going on for what seems like eons to them.

The Soul Watchers are animals in various forms from your past, present and future. They consist of the animals you care for, other domestic and livestock animals you encounter, wild animals, animal guides or those that represent the "essence" of animals. You may even refer to some of these animals as messengers. You will learn more about them in the next chapter.

Why do the animals refer to themselves as soul watchers? They have been watching the development of our souls for years. Humans have free will, and we can choose to allow the animals into our lives or not.

Even if we invite animals into our lives, we can choose their help—or not. Hence, the "watcher" role. Of course, the animals desire to take a more active role than that and hope you will take them up on their offer. They have quite an in-depth and diverse perspective of life, more so than we do, and are capable of teaching us profound life lessons.

Over time, animals have watched the destruction of their species, humanity and the world, our beautiful Mother Earth that we all share. They have been on a life-long mission to change this. Animals offer hope, wisdom, and guidance. In a world filled with chaos, they are humanity's best hope. WE are their mission. Animals live and "work" from their heart and soul. They are trying to reach and teach us on a body, mind, and spirit level. You see, humans often do more for the animals in their lives than they do for themselves or others. Animals are aware of this and try to utilize this to their advantage.

The animals have ancient wisdom that has been passed down through the ages. This sacred knowledge is from the animal collective, nature and Mother Earth. The animals know that some people have blinders on—and wish not to know more than they already do, for that is their current path. And they understand other people simply do not know what they do not know, but are really interested in knowing when given the opportunity.

Animals also realize that people live in a constant state of fear to some degree. After all, it's human nature. We can feel lost, confused. We may be worried or have anxiety. My massage therapist asked me once "How is that worrying going for you?" as she massaged my overly-tense muscles.

We can fear the unknown, the "what ifs." Fear paralyzes. Regardless of how fear manifests in our life, it prevents us from accessing the ability to grow and find our way. One of my teachers taught me years ago, FEAR is False Evidence Appearing Real. The animals want to help us know what they know, but also help us conquer our fears. They want to assist us in our becoming enlightened and empowered. You can even think of them as your personal buddhas, zen masters or yes, even Yoda.

The animals bring people together and unite us as one with all there is. Doe, the deer referred to this as the "Buddha Beam." This is the life force that is connected to everything in the universe and connects us all. You can think of this as harmonious beams of light. You can also view this as: we are all connected by an intricately woven spider's web, where the delicate filaments reach from one soul to another, all equally vital in this web of life.

This imagery reminds me of an incredible sweat lodge experience I had. I saw a vision of a faceted crystal. Inside the crystal appeared a spider web. And inside the spider web was a human eye. Then, that eye morphed into different species of animal eyes. We are all truly connected.

The animals have unconditional love and will give their life for us, even for reasons *out of this world.* I never cease to be amazed by their endless love and tireless efforts. Gabby is a good example of this love.

A friend and student of mine, asked if I would speak to Gabby, her cat. Her precious feline wasn't that old and passed away unexpectedly. What Gabby told me blew me away. When I asked why she left suddenly, she told me that she needed to go to help stabilize the moon. (Speaking to animals is discussed in chapter 6.)

I knew some animals were capable of shutting their bodily functions down and leaving, but I had no clue what "stabilize the moon" could possibly mean. I knew from my astrologer friend, Laura, that the moon, sun, and planets affected life here. I recall even how one of my vets would not schedule any castrations on a full moon, because there was a risk of increased blood flow and possible complications. I reached out to Laura, and she let me know that it made total sense based on events at the time. She was so honored by what Gabby did, and being a fellow cat lover herself, contacted her pet parent to shed more light on this.

The animals know that if they can impart some of their knowledge to you, that it will stir your heart and soul and change your life. They are here in different forms to help awaken you on a mental, physical, emotional and spiritual level. This includes taking you to your next level of consciousness. These gentle soul watchers can lead you on a sacred journey to your true, soul path.

The animals hold the hope for humanity in their hearts. For if they can make an impact on you, they know you hold the key that can make an impact on others.

ACTION: *Download the guide now, so you can start this journey together with the animals. Make a list of all of the domestic, livestock and wild animals that have been a part of your life now and in the past. Recall even the smallest moments in time when you had a special encounter with an animal.*

Chapter 2

The Soul Watchers Unite

> *Look inside. Look outside. For the answers are there,*
> *right in front of you. We are here for you. All creatures*
> *are here for you. We are here when you least expect it*
> *and when you need us the most. Don't be afraid*
> *to explore the animal world. We are all united in love*
> *and light. It is our honor to serve you.*

—ANGEL, MY HUSKY-CHOW IN SPIRIT

Now let's look at the ways the animals try to reach you, as it goes far beyond your own companion animals or those you may refer to affectionately as pets. Even if you have never cared for a pet, you still have animals who try to guide you in various ways.

Domestic and Livestock Animals

The most common way animals have to reach and teach us is as domestic and livestock animals that you care for or have encountered. They may be living in your home or belong to a family member, friend, or neighbor. These animals may even be under casual circumstances, such as a dog you pet at the dog park or a galloping horse you see while driving down a country road. Keep in mind these are animals in your life right now or have been in the past. They can include animals in spirit. Yes, animals who have crossed the Rainbow Bridge were with you for a reason and can still help to guide you.

Wild Animals

During your life, you have experienced times with wild animals. From the bee to the dragonfly to the cardinal in your own yard. Perhaps you have seen hawks, eagles, wolves, coyotes, bison, deer, snakes, whales, dolphins, crabs and so forth. You may have visited a state or national park, wildlife sanctuary or zoo. These encounters may have been brief, or you might have seen a specific species on a consistent basis, or even a regular visitor. At our first Texas home, we were delighted to have a mourning dove that returned year after year to build her nest in a window planter box on the front porch. We got to see many new lives emerge.

However, there are wild animals that don't ever come in contact with people, even from a distance, or may never be seen at all. But it is important to know that they all have a purpose. Animals can also contribute to the collective of that species.

Animal Guides

There are animals that are unique guides. A guide may be a real animal, such as your own or a wild one, but guides can also be an animal in an energetic form. Some refer to these guides as animal spirit guides. The "spirit" description does not mean the animal has passed on. This simply means this guide is more spiritual in nature because only the energy or essence of that animal comes through—there is nothing most are able to touch or truly see in reality. These guides can be a particular species, or they may be a type of animal you can't really identify. It does not matter what they look like. It only matters why they are here for you and what you have to learn from them. Keep in mind, guides can be in your life for a brief moment or a lifetime.

If you are passionate about a particular species of animal such as a lion, wolf or bear, this animal may very likely be an animal totem for you. Animal totems are guides that tend to help you throughout your life and can be any species, wild or domestic. This goes back to Native American beliefs, and the personal totems that guided and protected each individual. You can visualize them in your own personal animal totem pole.

My main animal totems are wolves, horses and humpback whales, and I've felt like kindred spirits with them since I was young. For animals you are drawn to, you may try to surround yourself with them in any way you can—animals you provide care for, those you view in nature, or objects such as books, figurines, clothing, jewelry, etc. And this attraction may have been on-going for years and even feel magical to you.

Receiving Messages

While sometimes, we can miss the boat when it comes to understanding the guidance from our own animals, most people aren't aware of the efforts these other animal guides make through various signs. So, they never receive their messages. It's easy to overlook a message from an animal guide or totem if you don't know what to look for. For instance, imagine one evening while driving, an owl flies near your vehicle. Unless you normally see owls, and they normally fly near you, then you would look at this as a sign of their attempt to reach you.

There may be an animal you regularly see but under unusual circumstances. I normally would see various types of bees on my farm when I lived in Texas, but one day, a wasp had made it into my bathroom. Sometimes a wasp would be by the back door, but my bathroom was at the far end of the house. This wasp was trying to reach me—but I didn't pick up on it at that time. A sure indication of a sign is a repetition of appearances by a particular species of animal. After I had gathered the wasp and released it outside, I didn't think more of it. But the very next day a wasp of a different coloration appeared in my bathroom.

I should have then realized the wasps needed to give me a message—but still I did not. So yes, the very next day another wasp of yet another color was there in my bathroom. Then it was like a 2x4 hit me over my head. I released that wasp and right away went to pursue their message for me. At the time, I was considering the possibility of asking someone to come teach Sacred Geometry to my family and students. Turns out this wasp wanted me to put this idea in action.

Repetitions of animals may happen in different ways. You might see a cheetah bumper sticker one day, then a billboard with a cheetah the next day, and a magazine ad that featured a cheetah the following day. In this case, the animals have not appeared in real form, but other ways in a short time span to get your attention. Even like this, they are indeed trying to reach you.

Other ways animals may try to reach you are through license plates, street signs, business names, songs, the radio, etc. The opportunities are endless, but the key is to notice a pattern of frequency for a particular animal species.

Nobody likes to see a dead animal on the side of the road or the life of one be taken. An animal may hit your vehicle like a dragonfly upon your windshield, or you may accidentally run over a darting squirrel in the road. While this is a sad experience, unless your vehicle is normally an animal magnet, this is a sign that an animal spirit wants to get a message to you. And yes, animals will give their life to give us messages. It can also be an animal you see on the side of the road that has already passed. Again, unless you usually see dead opossums on the side of the road for instance, then you would want to seek the message from that animal.

Another way that departed wild animals may try to reach you is through biofacts: objects such as horns, fur, feathers, shells, etc. that once belonged to a living animal. These objects still contain the energy or essence of that animal. Animals can still be of service in this fashion. When you find something of this nature on a walk, perhaps you will think twice about what that moment means and pursue it.

Animals can also alarm you with what I call "near misses." There was a mockingbird near my home that just loved to swoop right in front of my vehicle when I would drive back from my work at the zoo. This went on for over a year. It worried me greatly, as I was so afraid I would hit her. After several times of this action, I looked up the message, and I realized it was all about me speaking up in regards to my business. It was about me, not only embracing my voice, but sharing it with those that wanted to listen, like people who found our website, those on our email list, and our students. I needed to speak from the heart and be authentic to who I was. No holding back.

A week or a month could pass by. She would then swoop and land in a tree on the other side of the road. I would tell her, "I know. I know. Yes, I will work on speaking my truth, but please don't keep risking your life for me." Eventually, I made progress to her satisfaction. She stopped her daredevil flights, and I could breathe a sigh of relief for all of those times she risked her life for me. I was forever grateful for her commitment as she always came at times when I really needed encouragement.

You may also have animals reach out to you in dreams, visualizations, meditations, and what I like to refer to as holographically. The latter normally occurs when you are in bed but not asleep yet. When the animal appears, it looks lifelike, as if you could touch it.

My husband and I dreamed for years of moving from Houston to be near Yellowstone. My first holographic image did more than startle me. I had gotten into bed and settled down to go to sleep, but I wasn't there yet. I tend to fall asleep within 5 minutes. All of a sudden, a huge tarantula dropped down from the ceiling above my bed! It was so real and even larger than the goliath bird-eating tarantula at the zoo where I worked. I quickly jumped out of bed and threw on the light. Of course, there was no tarantula. I wondered if this would be a recurring experience, and while I loved arachnids, that was an unsettling thought.

On yet another night, my friend, the tarantula appeared to crawl down from the bedside lamp; and another time, made her way down the Yellowstone painting on the nearby wall. I looked up the message of the spider and understood that she was trying to reassure me that I am the weaver of my own life, and that I needed to have patience but put my ideas and plans into motion. The filaments would then reach out as they needed to. The tarantula would continue to visit me over the coming years, whenever I needed a friendly reminder and encouragement. She has even made a house call once at my home in Montana near Yellowstone, as I was getting settled into my new life.

Should an animal reach out to you like this, please don't be afraid. They are here to help you.

How to Decipher Messages

So how do you know what the animal's message is for you? There are a number of ways you can find out. The easiest way is to look it up on the internet. For instance, if a raccoon tries to reach you, look up the phrase "raccoon animal totem." It does not matter if you don't consider them a totem, but that is the terminology to bring you the results you need to determine their message for you. You will find different websites when you search. Look at the information until you find the message that resonates with you. This message can be about anything on a personal or professional level. It could be about your health, finances, relationships, work, etc. It may only be one sentence on the entire page, but you will know when you read it.

Another way is to look up the message in a book. I have the books *Animal-Wise* and *Animal Speak* by the late Ted Andrews. There are a number of animal guidebooks on the market. I used to have many more books but downsized my collection when we moved. You can also research the message in a card deck. Most have books or booklets that accompany the cards. I love the first animal card deck with book I ever got, *Medicine Power: The Discovery of Power Through the Ways of Animals* by Jamie Sams and David Carson. The book is sold separately by some, so if you want the cards, make sure you get the cards and book together. There are a growing number of different card decks available. I have quite a few. With card decks and books, the animal you seek might not be featured in them, and so the internet provides easy access to information.

Seeking Guidance

Besides animals that reach out to you, you can call on them in a variety of ways any time you want guidance. You can set your intention on a question or situation you have and ask to have an animal or particular guide to come forward to assist you. The more specific you are with your request, the better. If you have a specific animal in mind and have a photo of it, you can look at the photo. Otherwise, a photo of the animal is not necessary, as it is your intention that matters.

Let's say you want to connect with a sea turtle to find out what direction you should take with your career. You can say silently or out loud for example, "I want to connect with a sea turtle to determine if I should apply for the current supervisor promotion at work." Either a sea turtle you have seen before or a representative of that species will come forward. You can then draw a card, turn to a page in a book, or look online to see what message they have for you. Another option to connect with animals is to meditate and ask an animal to come forward that wants to help you, or you can call on a guide or specific species. Remember to be detailed in the guidance you are asking for. If you meditate with the sea turtle, you may feel or see things. You might get a warm feeling or a sense of peace in response to your request that you feel indicates a positive response. Or you might get a feeling of nervousness or anxiety that you might take as a sign to pass on the promotion. While meditating, you might see an image of the sea turtle. He may move his flippers excitedly, expressing you should go for it. Or he may swim away to let you know now is not the right time or perhaps not the right position for you—or on a deeper level, not the right company or even profession for you.

But only further exploration would allow you to know the answers to the "why"—or should I say "tangible" answers, as you probably know the why in your heart.

You can also ask an animal to give you three signs in a particular time period, such as a week for a "yes" response to whatever it is you seek guidance on. Remember to provide as much information as possible about what you want an answer to, and make sure what you are asking is a yes or no question. Keep in mind all of the ways animals may reach out to you, so you don't overlook their responses. If you see the three signs you requested, then you have your "yes." If you do not, it could be a "no," but it could also be that you did not provide enough details or that you simply overlooked the signs. You can certainly try again and see what happens.

The soul watchers work together collectively, as a team, to accomplish their mission. They are trying to reach YOU and want you to receive their messages. The animals also want you to know they are there for you, whenever you want to call on them. Hopefully, this will help you to be more cognizant about their efforts in your life. You will be amazed at what you can learn from them. It really is quite profound when you understand the vast expanse of the animal world on this type of level. Know they have always been there for you, but most people do not realize the animals can help in such incredible ways.

ACTION: *Previously, you made a list of animals that were part of your current and past life. Add any more that you may have thought of. Now, include animals that came to you in other ways, such as dreams, meditations, biofacts, etc. Write down any messages you were aware of at the moment or after a time of reflection, and any messages that come to you now as you go through the list of animals.*

Chapter 3

The Soul Watchers' Life Lessons

*All creatures great and small, for we all have something
to share with you. A powerful lesson can come from
a tiny animal, even an ant. Pay attention to the smallest
sound, the gentlest touch, the subtlest sensation,
the simplest words, the briefest moment. We are trying
to reach you in our own special way.*

—CINNAMON, MY GUINEA PIG IN SPIRIT

Animals teach us many lessons. Sometimes, the lesson
is about them. Other times, the lesson is about us. But no
matter what, they are lessons the animals want us to take
to heart and soul.

Soul Purpose and Soul Contracts

You have an important role in this universe, as does each animal. Every person and animal has a primary purpose in this life. This is referred to as their soul purpose. Your path is meant to cross with certain animals directly and others indirectly. As you strive to accomplish your soul purpose, your soul contracts play out.

Soul contracts are contracts animals and people have made as to which significant animals and people they will encounter in life and which crucial experiences they will have together. Soul contracts include what life lessons people and animals will experience. Contracts include those that involve health, relationships, careers, finances, etc. Think of a soul contract as a type of agreement between two souls.

There will be soul contracts you will have with specific animals. For instance, you could have a soul contract with your dog that they are going to bring joy, love and support into your life at a time you experience a great loss. This dog may be with you for fifteen years until they pass. Some animals are with you for just a short time. For example, you may have a contract with a cat that is going to introduce you to the love of your life, but only be with you for a brief time, and then leave your yard one day to seek their next contract with another person.

There are animals you may feel are one in a million. You could have animals your whole life, but you will probably only have one, or perhaps a few, that you consider to have a deep, soul connection with. You may refer to these animals as your "soul" or "heart" animal. More than likely, these animals have been with you in this lifetime or a previous lifetime, and that's why you feel this undeniable bond that probably seems stronger than your connection with other animals. I've been blessed with several of these heart and soul relationships: My first dog, Diamond, I had when I was ten to my early twenties, Rain, my wolf dog that was in my life for too short a time, and Tara, my 29-year-old horse that I've had since she was a yearling.

ACTION: *Take a look at the list of animals you have created. Write down about the soul contracts you feel you may have or have had with any of the animals. Include which animals you feel are your "heart" or "soul" animals.*

The Healing Touch

Animals can provide us with simple but important elements of life, such as companionship, joy, laughter, love, hope, peace and protection. Animals can also offer us healing. I like to call these animals healers, as that is one of the roles they play in life. Perhaps you've heard of the animals that visit hospitals and know exactly which patients they need to see, or the animals that can detect cancer, seizures, low blood sugar or other health conditions in humans.

Your animal may take drastic measures to alert you to a possible life-threatening situation. When Kate was out for a walk with Baron, her German shepherd, he tripped her, and she fell hard to the ground. This was so unlike him. Kate had to go to the doctor, and it was discovered that she had a blood clot in her right leg. Blood clots are potentially dangerous. Had Baron not injured her, this clot probably would have gone unnoticed. Kate feels in her heart that Baron saved her life.

Some animals want to help other people. When I taught Reiki, a form of energy healing, Lady, my terrier/chihuahua mix (pictured here), would sometimes jump up on the massage table when a student laid on it. For instance, she would sit on their hand or place her rear by their forehead or hip. When we started to notice this behavior, I asked each student if they knew why she did this. Turns out, every one of them had some kind of recent injury or condition and at that moment, experienced pain. Lady knew exactly where they needed help. She offered them healing energy from her own body.

I tell students that if your animal sits on your feet or lays at the foot of the bed by your feet, they are probably trying to help ground you. Unless of course, you have foot troubles, and then they may be trying to help you with that. If you aren't familiar with the term grounding, it is the feeling and act of being present and in the moment, secure and connected to the energy of Mother Earth. If your animal lays on or against you, ask yourself does this correlate to anything you know going on in that area of your body. If you are not aware of anything, keep an eye on that part of your body. Your animal may just want to use you as a cushion but perhaps, they know something that you don't.

Was Lady trying to give back for being adopted? Perhaps. But each animal has something special to offer in their own way. And some animals just happen to have the role to comfort other animals and help them get well. Mr. Handsome was one of those. He was an incredible blue Andalusian rooster that lived in the petting area at the Houston Zoo. He was the only rooster and kept the company of hens, goats and sheep.

I noticed something very interesting about him. He would walk along the top of the fence around the yard as if patrolling it. He was a rooster, and one might think he was simply on guard. But he was doing something else besides a patrol. Every time there was a sick animal, he would watch over it and try to comfort it. He didn't just extend this service to the hens. He would stand on the ground next to a sick or injured goat or sheep. I felt Mr. Handsome tried to be near the animal to offer them healing energy. He knew when an animal needed special attention, perhaps veterinary care. He had such compassion for his fellow friends.

I spoke to him often. I told him how special he was, and that it was so kind of him to give of himself to the animals that needed assistance. Every now and then, zoo visitors would even notice his unusual behavior, and I let them in on his little secret. Mr. Handsome continued this caregiver role for many years, until his passing. I will never forget his kind and gentle spirit. Indeed, healers can come in many shapes and forms.

ACTION: *Write down any experiences you have had where you feel an animal might be trying to heal you, an animal, or someone else.*

Forever Yours, Forever Mine

So many animals don't realize that you are giving them a forever home, even if you've had them for years. If your animal is adopted or you rescued them, it's very likely they have some type of emotional baggage. Some animals wonder if this is their last day with you. You can imagine how unsettled you would be to live like this. To feel like you don't have a real home or don't belong is hard for both people and animals. Often, this manifests in the form of anxiety or even aggression. It is fear based.

You can tell your animal out loud that they have a forever home, that you are their forever person, and they are safe and secure and will be with you no matter where you are. When an animal knows in their heart that they are forever yours, their fears can be alleviated. If you foster an animal or volunteer at an animal shelter, let that animal know of your search for a wonderful, forever home for them. They need to have hope, especially if they have been there for a long time or have been returned.

Ben was a husky that was rescued and lived in Sandra's home with other adopted dogs. He kept to himself and didn't seem happy even after one year of being there. Sandra then told Ben he had a forever home and would stay with her wherever she was. For the first time ever, he wagged his tail, as he finally knew his fate.

To further help animals, especially those with anxiety, tell them when you leave your house or facility and when you plan to return. For instance, you can tell them you'll be back in several hours or at dinner time. If you are gone for more than a day, let your animal know when you'll return. You can even say you'll come back after two suns or three moons. It can help to envision this in your mind and send them an image of what you want to tell them. You can set your intention to talk to your animal no matter where you are in the world. Connect your heart to their heart and envision a beautiful light or cord that connects your hearts together. You can even picture your light or cord with a specific color such as lavender or gold. Then picture your animal in your mind and start to talk to them. You can look at their photo if you want to. They will hear you! (We'll discuss this more in chapter 6.)

ACTION: *Write down the animals that you need to tell that they have a forever home, or that you are on the search for helping one find a forever home. Then do it.*

Look in the Mirror

Did you know that animals can mirror you? If you have an animal that has health or behavioral issues, it could be because you had this condition first, and they want to get you to help them with hopes that you will eventually help yourself. Animals know that most humans will do more to help them than people will often do to help themselves. The animals also realize that when you take action to help them, you then understand better how to help yourself. When we help them to heal, we have the knowledge to heal ourselves.

While it may be easier to understand how an animal would feed off of your own emotions and react, they can also mirror you with physical conditions. My business partner, Allison, told her neighbor, Ruth, that she would take her calico cat, Saucey, when she found out that Ruth didn't have long to live. Saucey was not that old, yet the vet had to do a lot of chiropractic adjustments on her. Saucey was arthritic. What was Ruth's condition? Sadly, she had bone cancer. Saucey was doing her best to help Ruth's health. One day, we asked Dr. Tom, a small animal veterinarian, if he noticed with his animal cancer cases, if any of the pet parents also had cancer. He thought about it and realized yes, there were some with cancer. It was as if a light bulb went off for him. Animals do this out of love for us.

Most illness and disease are a result of unaddressed or buried emotions for both animals and people. And what's interesting is that the energetic nature of the condition can manifest in the energy field before it can be detected by routine diagnostic tests such as blood work, urinalysis or radiographs. Animals often know what is going on in their body or yours before you or someone else realizes it.

If you think your animal has taken on an issue of yours, tell them you wish that they release it. It's very likely that your animal's actions were due to their soul contract with you. You can let your animal know that you appreciate their devoted efforts and will try to improve the situation. Then do your best to support your animal and yourself on a body, mind, and spirit level.

ACTION: *Write down if you feel any animals are presently mirroring you or another family member physically or emotionally. Think about the message they have for you and write it down. Then take action. Write down if you feel any animals were mirroring you or a family member in the past. Determine if you feel this is resolved for those involved. If it was not resolved, write down action steps.*

The Yellow Brick Road

Not every health or behavioral issue for animals is due to mirroring. Your animals try to teach you, including the courage to believe in them and stand firm in your own beliefs.

Princess was a beautiful dog diagnosed with a brain tumor. Jennifer took her to radiation treatments and felt it was going well. Princess had a good appetite throughout this and even though tired at times, had a strong will to live. Jennifer's friends told her they felt what she was putting Princess through was cruel and that she should end her dog's suffering. One of her friends was even a well-known and respected animal communicator. Princess' holistic vet felt the treatments were going well and could extend the dog's life by at least six months.

Furthermore, she felt Princess had strong *chi*, the life force in our bodies. For Jennifer, she wanted as much time as possible with her beloved dog. However, even though she felt what she was doing was right in her heart, she was torn about whether to proceed with the last week of radiation treatments because of what her friends had said. Jennifer's vet encouraged her to contact me before she made a decision. I used muscle testing to determine what holistic methods would help Princess the most. Energy work and a custom Bach flower essence blend showed up strongly (more about those in the next chapter). Princess muscle tested for the color yellow, to bring sunshine and joy into her life. When I was at Jennifer's home, I was able to teach her how to offer energy work to Princess. I also noticed the red décor in her home. The color red can agitate and possibly cause cancer cells to spread. So, Jennifer worked on a new look. Princess finished her treatments and several years later, was still going strong! No cowardly lioness here!

ACTION: *Write down any experiences where an animal has given you courage in some way or may be trying to do so now. Act on this if possible.*

Listen Closely

When an animal continues to act out or have health conditions, this can indicate that you haven't gotten the message they want to teach you. Cindy's grey Persian cat, Samantha, repeatedly urinated on her bed or suitcase whenever she had to go out of town, which created quite the mess. A trip to the vet ruled out a possible physical health issue. It turned out that Cindy's schedule constantly changed, and she didn't spend that much time with her cat. When Cindy started to tell Samantha when she would leave home and when she planned to return, and in addition, spend more time with her, the inappropriate behavior stopped. So, when you see your animal act naughty, ask yourself why they might behave this way. Most of the time, we do know the reason in our hearts. Sometimes though, we don't want to listen, especially if this turns out to be a reflection of us. Remember, most animals will be persistent in their efforts to reach you as that is part of their role in your life.

Mark had some potentially serious health problems but really didn't seem to focus on his own well-being. His palomino horse, Banjo, also had physical conditions, but different from Mark's. When Mark started to work on himself and make progress, Banjo's health started to improve. So, even though this wasn't a case of mirroring, it is an example of how an animal will do whatever they can to get their pet parent's attention. Animals can act out and exhibit health issues as a wake-up call for us. Some animals are able to make themselves sick if they feel it might help you receive their message—and act on it. If you just "know" and "acknowledge" their lesson, this often isn't enough. The animals want to see you put forth the time and energy to actually take care of yourself. They have such love for us and can be quite determined in their efforts to reach and teach us.

ACTION: *Write down any experiences where you think you have not gotten the message from an animal. Try to determine what that message is and write it down. Then try to act on it.*

Manifest Success

If an animal feels like you aren't connected with them or are not clear what you want them to do, they may have behavioral issues. Remember, emotional conditions can turn into physical problems when they aren't addressed. Make sure you tell your animals out loud what you want them to do, not what you don't want them to do. The mistake most people make is to tell their animal what they don't want them to do and use negative words such as "don't" or "no." Animals don't always pick up on these negative words, especially when humans are not happy, and they may only hear "pee on the carpet" instead of "don't pee on the carpet." Just as with your own intentions, negatives don't work. And when people speak like that to animals, they are probably unaware of the unintentional imagery they create in their mind of the animal doing the undesirable behavior. After all, this is human nature. And guess what? The animal can tune into the images you are projecting in your mind. Therefore, they think you want them to pee on the carpet.

So, you should always speak to an animal about what you want to see happen. When you want to manifest something in life, you focus on what you want to become a reality. It's no different if you want to have a wonderful relationship with animals. It helps to envision in your mind what you want them to do. You may want to surround your goal with a green bubble or color of your choice. If you can also offer your animal a positive reward for the behavior you desire, you'll make further progress. Keep in mind that if they are not food motivated, if they already receive a food treat, or if they prefer your attention over food, a regular treat is not going to do the trick.

Give some real thought as to what would make them the happiest, within reason, that you are willing to do. For example, if your dog is peeing on the carpet, tell your dog out loud you want them to pee on the grass and that they will get (the reward) if they go on the grass. Visualize in your mind that your dog has gone potty on the grass. When your dog uses the restroom on the grass, make sure you offer them the special reward you told them about. Otherwise, they will lose their trust in you, just like a child can with a parent that doesn't follow through. Remind your animal about what you want to see them accomplish until it becomes a habit. Just change this thought process on how you work with behavioral issues, and you'll have the potential to resolve many problems and deepen your animal's trust in you.

ACTION: *If you have a current behavioral issue, write down what you can say to your animal out loud, what you can think and visualize in your mind, and a possible reward. Then act on it.*

The Right Stuff

Animals come here with a purpose but want to see you act on this. If your animal seems confused or unfocused, it could be because they do not understand what place they have in your household or life, especially if you are a multi-person or animal home. For instance, are they your companion to hang out with, do you want them to be a protector, or do you want them to be a best buddy for another animal? It's easy for an animal to feel lost or unsure, especially if they were adopted or rescued. Make sure you tell them what role they have in your life. Explain to them in detail what that role looks like to you. Think of how it will manifest. What do you want to see from them?

Laddie was a young golden retriever that a boarding facility wanted to use for temperament testing of new dogs that applied for daycare. However, he tended to greet the dogs aggressively. It was explained to him out loud that he needed to be gentle and kind towards the other dogs. He was also told how he was chosen for this very special job and his pet parent wanted him to be a role model. Laddie's behavior changed, and he quickly improved to where he could be used for this important role. Just like children, animals can need to be reminded of what you spoke about. So, don't be afraid to talk regularly with your animal. In fact, this is what your animal wants.

Most people do some "small talk" with their animals like "Hi there" or "Mommy's home now." But animals want far more than this. They want you to speak to them as if they're an important part of your life. Tell them about how your day went, when you are sad, when you are in pain. Tell them your hopes and dreams. Speak from your heart. Your animals want you to share this with them. You'll be amazed at the difference it can make in your relationships with animals when you include them more in your life. (We'll touch on this more in chapter 6.)

ACTION: *Write down any animals that you feel need to be told their role in your life. Write down what that role is in detail and then share it out loud with them.*

The Winner's Circle

Over the years, we've had clients wonder if their animals enjoy particular activities or competing in events. Sometimes, pet parents choose sports or have a competitive drive for what they want to do, not necessarily what the animal cares to do. It's important to take their desires into consideration. After all, it's fun if you can have fun together. Animals want to please us so are often willing to do anything we drag them into. But ultimately, that doesn't make for the best of relationships. It can even contribute to behavioral issues. If your animal seems reluctant, unfocused, withdrawn, rowdy or simply unhappy, chances are they probably are. This just isn't their cup of tea, so to speak. Even if they win blue ribbons for you, some animals could care less about that. On the other hand, there are those that can't wait to be in the spotlight. But if you look into your animal's heart, you will know their true wishes.

If what you do, though, is something you have your heart set on, then tell them why this is so important to you. Really talk to them about why this means so much to you and what you want the outcome to be with them. This literally could change their mind and motivate them. On the other hand, perhaps they just want to go on a casual walk or trail ride with you and not have some set agenda, at least not all of the time. Maybe you can find a balance. Ask yourself if they seem happy doing this activity or competition with you. If not, it's time to reevaluate things and find something you and your animal can enjoy together, as equal partners.

Sara loved showing her afghans. Missy was very beautiful in the show ring, but she started to seem withdrawn and not her usual self. Sara wondered if Missy had something wrong with her or if she no longer enjoyed herself. After we tuned in and spoke with Missy (we'll discuss this in chapter 6), we found out that she really didn't want to be a show dog but didn't want to disappoint Sara. Sara wanted to honor Missy's wishes, so she decided they would do fun activities together they both enjoyed. Missy's "go getter" personality quickly returned.

The same philosophy goes for breeding animals. I bred collies for many years, and they sold like hotcakes because so many families wanted a Lassie of their own. I was oblivious to their emotional needs, except to help me make money. I even offered a collie stud service when I was just 14. My dogs helped to provide me with income in my earlier years. In my bedroom, I still have a gorgeous pine cabinet I had custom built for myself when I was 18.

My horses have had some children of their own. In fact, Tara, my 29 year-old mare, lives with her first offspring,

Rosa, who is 24 years old (both pictured here). Their bond is incredible, and I realize how blessed they are to have one another.

But since that time, I have come to have a different mindset and a different understanding about breeding. If you breed, do you have a wait list for your animals, or might you need to find homes for some of them? You certainly don't want to intentionally contribute to the overpopulation and euthanization of animals. Did you ever think to consider if your animal wants to be bred? Did you take into consideration what it's like for a mother to lose her children? These are questions I wish I had asked myself.

Animals are like us. Some women want to have children, and others can't fathom the idea of it. Not every animal wants to be a parent. And when their children go off to new homes or pass away, how does that make them feel? Some may feel overjoyed that they are moving out, but other animals are going to worry about their offspring or feel a sense of loss.

If you breed animals now or want to consider it, take a close look at how your animals "handle" the situation. Speak to them about this role in their life. Determine if they really should be bred. When their young pass away, let them say goodbye and console them. When their children go to a new home, let your animal know how carefully you have screened the new parents to determine that they are able to provide a wonderful new life. If you take this compassionate approach to breeding, you will notice a positive change in your animals, and even yourself.

ACTION: *Write down any animals you need to speak to about their desires for activities, competitions or breeding. Write what you want to say to them, and then share it with them.*

Think Outside the Box

Sometimes things are not as they appear or what we may think. One of the biggest reasons that cats end up in shelters, or worse, is because they don't use the litter box. We have worked with so many cats, and this experience has been eye opening. Cats can act out like Samantha did because you don't communicate or spend enough time with them. But felines can be opinionated and even come across as arrogant at times. There are many reasons why they won't use the litter box. The box could be the wrong color, style, height or location. The litter may be the wrong type, amount or not cleaned often enough. Cats may even despise the mat you placed in front of the box, because it feels funny on their feet. Then there are the personality clashes. They may not want to share the box or like that there's another cat in their home. It's always important to get your cat checked out by a vet to rule out possible health issues. But most of the time, you'll find your cat is not using the litter box because they are unhappy for some reason, and there's a good chance it's something you have done, or not done, unintentionally. Cats are very clever at doing their best to set you on the right path, albeit their tactics may be forceful at times.

ACTION: *Write down any animals that you should think outside the box about. Write down possible actions you can take, and then act on them.*

To Be or Not to Be

Animals teach us to be careful about passing judgement. Some animal lovers feel that animals in captivity, such as zoos, have horrible lives. Having worked for a world-class zoo for many years, I can tell you that those animals had the best possible care. Now, were all of the animals happy to be there? No, they were not. Some of them had no choice because they were injured and couldn't be released into the wild. And some animals would have been euthanized if our zoo hadn't given them a home. Some just didn't want to be in captivity. It's true, not all zoos are the same, especially roadside zoos, where the care is not up to par. But did you ever think of the animals in homes, rescues or sanctuaries? Not all of those animals are happy, either.

Did you ever think that when an animal escaped, they did so for a reason? Keep in mind that animals come into this life for a reason. They have a specific purpose, and they're aware of precisely what those major roles entail before they are even born. It may be the role of a zoo animal, companion animal, working animal, etc. And if that dog runs away from its pet parent or foster family, it could be because it's time for it to move onto its next home—that there is somebody else it is supposed to be with at that time in its life. While most animals want to return home, and energy should be spent to find a lost animal, keep in mind that some are headed out on a road trip to their next destination.

ACTION: *Write down any animals you feel that could have moved on because they had another role to fill. Allow yourself to know in your heart that they left for a reason.*

Rainbow Bridge Surprises

Animals can choose their time to cross the Rainbow Bridge. Just like they chose to be with you, they can choose when they need to leave. Each animal has their own path, like you do. Some animals leave as a collective, like a large group of dogs or cats leave because they are needed on the other side. Some depart because they know they'll be able to help you more on the other side with their spiritual guidance. Many pet parents wonder what they can do to help their animals when the Rainbow Bridge is near. But sometimes, animals want you to do something that has nothing to do with them.

Sharon's black lab, Tippy, had reached the end of her journey. Sharon wanted to know what she could do to help her beloved dog. Right away, when Allison connected to Tippy, she got an image of a goose in her mind. When she told Sharon about this image, Sharon knew immediately what that meant. You see, Sharon's mother was referred to as the duck lady, because she had many ducks. And yes, geese and ducks can appear similar in an image. And it turns out, Sharon and her mother had not spoken in seven years. What did Tippy really want at the end of her life? To see Sharon and her mother reunited. Because this is what Tippy truly desired, Sharon honored her wishes and reconnected with her mom. This was the continuation of a relationship that is still strong, today. When we open our hearts, we can see the desires of our animal's heart. In honoring their wishes, we are filled with life's riches. The animals want us to be happy, and they understand the value of human relationships. And sometimes, that is their last wish for us.

When it comes time to say goodbye, there is one thing that remains clear and true. No matter what, no matter how, the animals are ready to leave and cross the Rainbow Bridge, whether they are able to do so on their own or with some help. They do not wish us to feel guilty in any way.

We touched earlier on Jack departing to help the moon. Animals are truly self-less and at times, we don't realize the sacrifices they make. Susie lost her sister at a young age, got divorced, lost her job, and had become very bitter. When she got a white, toy poodle puppy named Tanner, he changed her life. She started enjoying life. She walked him and interacted with neighbors. Years passed and Susie developed some serious health issues. She had heart surgery, followed by another heart attack and several strokes that impaired her vision. Even though frailty took over, she still tried to walk Tanner as much as possible. He was her rock.

One day, Susie walked Tanner down their usual path but on this occasion, several dogs got out of the gate of an elderly couple down the street. The large dog grabbed Tanner with his mouth and shook his little body. Susie was able to get Tanner away from the dog and rush him to the vet. The vet was unable to find any injuries, and Susie took Tanner home that night. Susie and Tanner slept together, touching each other all night as they had done every night for years. When Susie awakened the next morning, Tanner was no longer alive. Sadly, he passed during the night.

Susie was devastated. She had always told Tanner that she would be with him until the end and never leave him. Well, Tanner knew that Susie was very ill and might not be able to stay in her home much longer. If she had to go to a hospice facility, she would not be able to bring Tanner with her. Susie would have broken her promise to him, and he knew the guilt would be unbearable for her to live with. Tanner knew that if he left this earthly world before Susie, she could be at peace in her heart that *she never left him*.

Now, let's take a look at the carefully constructed plan Tanner had. First, the group of dogs that had gotten out had done so before several times, and only walked over to other dogs, greeted them with gentle sniffs, nothing more. Secondly, the vet found no injuries, which allowed Susie to spend the night peacefully with Tanner, touching him, instead of the need for him to stay in the animal hospital. Lastly, right after Susie had another mini stroke, she was not able to walk easily, or often. Tanner knew Susie felt guilty for not being able to care for him as she should and that her health was only going to decline.

While it's easy to think of this as a tragic story, we need to look at this as a gift. So many times, what we perceive as tragedy is actually a blessing to us from the animals.

ACTION: *Write down about any animals that crossed the Rainbow Bridge that you realize may have been a blessing in disguise.*

Too Much to Bear

Animals teach us to love, and they teach us to grieve. If you hear of someone else's story of their pet loss, this may bring you to tears. Grieving assistance has become more recognized with pet loss support groups. Holistic vets that offer in home euthanasia may also provide support afterwards for you and your family. It's very important to not only allow yourself to grieve, but extend this to family members.

If you have other animals, if possible, you want to allow them to say farewell before their friend passes and afterwards. If they didn't get to say goodbye, let them know what happened. Just like people, some animals may find it difficult to deal with the loss, including feeling guilty. When this happens, it's important to look into ways to support them through this grieving process and the release of any guilt. Some animals want a ceremony you can do together to provide peace and closure. You may want to post a photo or dedication to your animal on a pet memorial website. If you clear the "space" in your home and property with something like white sage, this can help remove the heavy energy from mourning. Simply light the sage and allow it to smolder. Set your intention to release this energy and fill the space with positive energy. You can say a prayer if you wish. Go around the outside of your home and the inside, and make sure you get into spaces such as closets.

During this challenging time, your animal may want you to spend more time with it. You may find comfort from one another. You may want to offer energy work, a custom flower essence blend or color therapy for your animals and yourself. The color yellow can be uplifting like sunshine or a beautiful sunflower. You can wear yellow clothing or jewelry. You can offer your animal a yellow towel or blanket to lay on or near.

Lavender, frankincense, rose, neroli, melissa, rosemary, bergamot and orange are essential oils that may help with grief. The easiest and safest way to offer aromatherapy is to just take the lid off of the bottle and let your animal smell as they desire. The homeopathic remedy Ignatia 30C potency can help animals and people overcome grief. (These various methods are discussed more in the next chapter.)

You and your animals should support each other. And if you lost your only pet, you may want to seek help, so that you don't feel alone during this difficult time.

ACTION: *Write down about any animals that you feel guilty about their passing or that you or your animals struggle with their loss. Write down steps you can take to relieve this guilt and grief. Start to take action.*

'Til Death Do Us Part

I have never liked this phrase. Simply because death is not the end. Sadly, there are those that think it is final. Yes, there is a physical death of the body. But the human and animal soul or spirit continues on. Our connection to our animals is everlasting. And what is really cool is that our animals will come visit us when they have passed. We just need to know to look for the signs.

Patty's beloved multi-color cat, LC (pictured here), passed away. She deeply missed him, especially since she has been challenged with many debilitating health issues. When I let Patty know about the signs to look for, she noticed LC would visit her whenever she wasn't feeling well. She could see indentations on her bed. She could feel him next to her. Sometimes, she could even see LC. When he visited, she enjoyed talking to him. Years later, Patty still lets me know that LC comes to see her, and she is forever grateful for his devoted love.

When animals return to visit, you may notice they have moved their toys or other belongings. You may see indentations on the bed, couch or other furniture. You may feel their body next to you or on you. You may even see glimpses of shadows, an outline or their physical body as they used to appear to you.

We have found that most animals want to return to their humans in physical form to continue on with the life they shared with you. Some of your animals have actually been with you before. They have shared a life or multiple lives with you, either during this lifetime or previous past lives. The movie *A Dog's Purpose* was about a dog that reincarnated and went through multiple dog lives with different owners to eventually return to the child he was with that was now an adult. Reincarnation is not fiction. It is reality. It does indeed happen. If you are not a believer, I encourage you to check on the internet about the myriad stories of the lifetimes young children remember. They are the best verified. There are also a number of animal reincarnation books available.

What's really neat is that when an animal passes away, you can actually find out if they will return to you and if so, when they plan to return and how you will know it's them! This is done through animal communication (more about that in chapter 6). Animals can give you an approximate time frame of when they will return. Keep in mind that this is based on how your life is going at this time. When that time comes, they may determine that this is not the ideal time in your life for them to come back. You can find out from them when the timing may be more ideal. We have found that most of the time, dogs will return as dogs and cats as cats, for instance. But it's possible a dog may become a cat or a cat a horse or another animal.

Your animal can shed light on how you will know it's them. They will normally tell you, or show you in your mind, what kind of animal they will return as and some kind of description or visual, such as a small brown dog with a short coat. They may indicate a sex, name, eye color, identifying marks, or even how you might find them. Keep in mind that names may be exact, but more likely they sound similar to the name you might discover them under, like Sally may be Shelly at the shelter. Animals may also share how you'll find them, such as they might show up at your front door, at a rescue group or shelter, or on a walk down the street.

Mike's dog, Rufus, had passed away. Rufus said that he would return in about a year and would look very similar to his brown and white coloring. Eleven months later, Mike ran an errand and from his car, saw a dog wandering through an empty, grassy lot. He couldn't believe his eyes, as it looked like Rufus. He parked his car and called out to the collarless dog. The dog came running towards him, as if he was reunited with his best friend. Rufus had indeed returned.

While most animals want to return to you, we have found that a small percentage are angels, or have another mission to take on and will remain on the other side. They can share with you what their role is beyond the veil—the afterlife. So, no matter what, just know in your heart that your animal lives on and will forever be connected to you in some way.

ACTION: *Write down about any animals that may have come to visit you and the possible signs you have encountered. Write down if you feel any animals you have now could be an animal from your past.*

Land of Lost Souls

It is not unusual for human and animal spirits to return to visit. However, some never leave. Buster was a beautiful, chestnut gelding that had badly injured himself. Jane felt something odd had happened to her horse and wanted to know what it was. When I connected to Buster, he shared with me that he had gotten spooked. I saw him frantically run and then stumble, which caused his body to flip and become injured. I could see the area where this happened. When I shared this information with Jane, she knew the location I spoke of and the description of the incident made sense with what she was saw with Buster's injuries. Jane then told me something I'll never forget.

It turns out their property used to be a game preserve before they bought it. Many animals were hunted on their land. Hence, many had perished tragically, and their spirits were lingering. This is what spooked Buster. When spirits like this remain, it creates negative energy. This is not the same as a beloved pet that passed and wants to visit. When negative energy is present, it can affect the physical, mental, emotional and spiritual well-being of the animals and people on the land. Land is sacred and this land was holding on to the past, unable to release it.

Sadly, Buster seemed to be amongst a large number of family animals that had been sick or injured over the years. Jane understood what she had to do. These animals needed to be able to finally move on in peace. Prayers for the animals that died needed to happen. A clearing and blessing of the land needed to take place as soon as possible. Buster had opened her eyes to the reality of what had been going on for ten long years.

Jane found someone local to help her with this crucial endeavor. After they were done, she told me something amazing happened. Jane could feel the darkness lift and apparently, so could the wild animals. For the first time ever since she lived there, a flock of wild turkeys appeared. And do you know what turkeys symbolize? They represent the honor of nature and Mother Earth through the development of a harmonious relationship with the land and those that reside there. Yes, the turkeys had spoken. The land was truly free at last. And with that, animals and people now had the opportunity to heal.

ACTION: *Write down if you feel there is any negative energy present in your home or on your property. Write down if you think this has possibly affected the physical, mental, emotional or spiritual well-being of any person or animal. Write down steps you can take to clear this energy and take action.*

This chapter represents just a sampling of the possible lessons that animals are trying to teach you. Whenever you wonder about the animals in your care, always ask yourself, "Could there be a lesson in this for me?" Do you need to take action for yourself? Do you need to take action for your animal? Think about the situation carefully and see if you can formulate some possibilities along with action steps to take.

Chapter 4

The Soul Watchers' Medicine Chest

*Humans must reconnect with nature to save themselves
and their homes. It is urgent. Holistic is a way of life.
Nature has so much to offer, that nurtures
your heart and soul.*

—RAIN, MY WOLF DOG IN SPIRIT

Wild animals rely on Mother Earth for survival. Their ancestral wisdom is encoded in domesticated animals. You could say they share the innate ability of how to utilize Mother Earth's medicine chest to help prevent illness and disease and heal on a physical, mental, emotional and spiritual level. And the animals truly wish the same for us. The information in this chapter is meant to be a general overview to help you understand the healing power of nature. Nothing in this book is meant to replace proper veterinary or medical care, but to present to you the knowledge of the animals.

Water Wisdom

Water is crucial to all life. Did you know that city or tap water contains chemicals and toxins such as chlorine, fluoride, arsenic, aluminum, copper, lead, mercury, nitrates, perchlorate, dioxins, PCBs (polychlorinated biphenyls), herbicides and pesticides? This water can cause all kinds of health issues for you and your animals. It is better to opt for purified, spring, filtered or good quality well water. If you are considering bottled water because of the danger that chemicals can leach from bottles into water, not to mention the environmental harm that bottles create, a water filtration system of some kind is ideal. You can look into a countertop filter, a faucet mount, an under the sink system, a water pitcher or even a water bottle with a filter.

We must stay hydrated to survive. Being hydrated helps us to be a healthier advocate for the animals and nature. But how much water should you and your animals drink? To say that every person should have 8 glasses of water a day or use a formula based on your weight is not necessarily accurate. Water needs are not only dependent on the health and activity level of each person and animal, but also on cellular hydration. Drinking more water does not equal proper hydration. You see, things like EMFs (Wi-Fi, electrical, power sources, etc.) and chemicals affect your and your animal's hydration on that cellular level.

Most humans probably don't drink enough. But, you can use muscle testing to determine how much water is right for you. (We will talk about muscle testing in the next chapter.) Monitor your animal's intake of water. Cats tend to derive much of their moisture from their food. Dogs may drink ½–1 ounce of water per pound. If you observe your dog or cat drinking too much water, this could indicate possible kidney or metabolic issues. Keep in mind that an all dry/kibble diet offers hardly any moisture and can be a huge detriment to the health of dogs and cats. They can't rely on water alone for proper hydration—they must also have the necessary moisture in their food. But water is important for all animals and drinking too much or too little could indicate potential problems.

Now that we've talked about water from a survival point of view, let's talk about it from a metaphysical approach. Water represents life and the flow of the collective unconscious. Water sounds are soothing and meditative. Water can receive, hold or clear energy. Flower and crystal essences, essential oils, and homeopathy are created with water.

While some health issues are a result of improper nutrition or environmental factors, it is thought that the majority of illness and disease is the result of unresolved emotional issues. It is believed that the possible cause of all negative emotions is a disruption in the body's energy system. Traditional Western medicine tends to focus more on the physical nature of the body and treats the symptoms. Holistic medicine is naturally derived from Mother Earth, and not only focuses on the physical aspect of the body, it also looks at the emotional side, a key factor in both prevention and treatment that goes to the root of the problem. Natural methods focus on aiding the body and its energy system, the primary source of physical and mental health issues for both people and animals.

To understand more about how this process works, Einstein's Theory of Relativity states that all physical matter is composed of energy. The science of quantum mechanics generally states that substance is simply vibration, in other words, the simplest form of energy.

Everything in the universe vibrates and has a unique frequency on an energetic level. Even water is sensitive to vibration. Water is a life force, and people and animals are composed mostly of water. So, what does this mean? If water is sensitive to subtle energy and people and animals are mostly water, then any energy-based method has the ability to have a *profound* impact on a physical, mental, emotional, or spiritual level.

Because animals and people are primarily water, the words that you speak and the thoughts that you think affect yourself and others on a cellular level. The power of water was revealed in Masaru Emoto's book, *The Hidden Messages in Water*. His revolutionary research proves that what you say, think, and hear affects the water in our bodies. It will make you think twice about what words come out of your mouth, what thoughts enter your mind and what you listen to, especially around your animals.

ACTION: *Take a look at your source of water and the amount of water you and your animals drink. Write down if this needs to be improved upon and steps you can take to do so. Reflect upon the metaphysical aspect of water and how it affects both people and animals on a cellular level. Write down your thoughts.*

The Sun and Moon Team

The sun and moon are more important to life than you may realize. The animals have this awareness and want to share it with us.

We need sunshine to survive, but there needs to be a balance of light and dark. The sun is thought to represent our conscious mind and inner strength. The sun can help us to understand our higher self and seek our soul purpose. Consider how we not only need the sun for physical reasons, but the impact it has on our emotional well-being. It is considered male energy or yang. Abundance, balance, clarity, confidence, prosperity, stability and truth are considered attributes of the sun. Solar eclipses and solar flares are both powerful and can affect life on Mother Earth in various ways. You may notice the energy from them affects you or your animals emotionally or physically.

The moon is believed to represent our unconscious mind, intuitive thinking and emotions. It is considered female/yin. You may have heard that the tides ebb and flow with the waxing and waning of the moon. The lunar cycle features moon phases that correlate with ideal time frames in which to accomplish specific endeavors. Here are some examples. The moon gets brighter during the waxing moon (as it gets bigger), so this is a great time to focus energy on your personal and professional goals. The illumination decreases during the waning moon, which indicates the time to contemplate your choices and to release whatever no longer serves you. During the "growing" new moon, you can set your intentions, start a new project or rebirth an old one. With the energy surge from the full moon, evaluate and recharge your life, and include a cleanse for yourself and your space (more about that in chapter 6). Most often when people and animals "react" to the moon, it's during a full moon or an eclipse. Dogs are especially known to have potty accidents or frenzied energy during this time.

I am very drawn to both the sun and the moon. When rays burst forth from the clouds, I like to call them sun beams or sun bursts. When they radiate across a great expanse, they are brilliant. I love to watch the moon and the changes it goes through. I remember looking at the moon with admiration when I was a young teen. I still do.

ACTION: *Write down any special experiences or thoughts you have about the sun or moon. Write about any reactions you have noticed with yourself or your animals to the sun or moon.*

Plants and Trees

When I was a young child in Houston, my brother and I went to a huge home and garden expo with our grandparents. One vendor was giving away a 45 record of loving words to play for your plants. We thought it was crazy but took one. How little did we know then the healing ability of plants and the power of actually speaking to them! Plants and trees deserve awareness and respect, just like animals. Animals know the amazing properties plants and trees have and want us to see the use of them in a new light. Nutrition, herbs, flower essences, aromatherapy, and homeopathy all utilize plants and/or trees in some way to create powerful tools for prevention and healing. We will touch on them separately.

Necessary Nutrition

We always say that without the proper nutrition, anything else you do is just a temporary fix. That goes for both people and animals. It's easy to think that if you feed a good holistic food to your animals, they receive what they need. We have found that most animals, even those on holistic diets, need their nutrition adjusted. It's one of the most popular consultations that we do, so we speak from years of experience where we have helped many animals through food. Remember, every animal is unique. It would be great if you could feed all of your animals the same way, but chances are, that's not going to work. And if you try to do that, you could end up shortening their life.

First, we will talk about the main basics to take into account when you evaluate what type of diet to feed your animal, which is important before you give them supplements:

Grains or No Grains—Grains play a vital role in many allergies and can contribute to chronic diseases such as diabetes and cancer. We have found that most dogs and cats do best on a grain free diet. Even some horses do. My horses were on soaked beet pulp for years, and this helped relieve inflammation in their bodies, but when we moved to Montana, with the harsher climate and their advanced age, they needed grains.

If your dog has kidney issues, they may need more grains than protein. Since cats are obligate carnivores, they may do very well on a raw diet. If your dog is on a grain free diet, Dr. Karen Becker, a well-known holistic veterinarian, recommends to add a weekly can of sardines to make sure they get enough taurine in their diet.

Best Type of Diet—You may be feeding all kibble, but did you know that it lacks the necessary moisture dogs and cats need? Dry food can damage their organs and especially kidneys over time. Raw can be best—but it's not appropriate for every animal or every pet parent. A cooked, dehydrated, canned or a can/kibble combo diet are better options than an all kibble diet. For livestock and other animals, you need to look at all the choices available, then go from there. Keep in mind that it's beneficial to divide an animal's diet up into two to three feedings a day, just like you would normally do for yourself.

Proteins—Did you realize that chicken and lamb are hot meats in Traditional Chinese Medicine (TCM)? This means they can heat up the body, which can cause inflammation. Your dog or cat may benefit from that, but many do not. Chicken is so cheap that it's put in so many brands of food. A number of holistic vets feel this has contributed to a fat imbalance among a large number of animals.

Look at what is going on with your animal. The key is to rotate the proteins—but use the ones that are best for your animal right now in their life. Turkey is cooling to the body. Beef and bison are considered neutral. Duck is cool, but because it tends to have fatty properties, based on what we've seen, most dogs and cats don't seem to do well on it. Fish tends to work well for many, but they have different properties depending on the type of fish.

Fruits and Vegetables—Feeding fruits and vegetables has become trendy. One of the problems is that they are fed raw or cooked, which is not processed enough for some animals. Let's think back to the wild animals. When they eat an herbivore's stomach content, it's in a digested format. If you feed pureed fruits and vegetables, this can help to cut down the chance that your animal's stomach may react poorly. But before you decide to feed any to your animal, know that fruits and vegetables have warm, cool and neutral properties, just like proteins do. So, ask yourself if you are doing more harm than good to your animal's body, because even pureed may have a negative effect.

Supplements—Once you've determined your animal's core diet, then and only then should you look at supplements. There are many animals on the wrong supplements, the incorrect amounts, or they are being over-supplemented, which can wreak havoc on their immune system. You may wonder why they can't get well. Let's look at some common supplements many animals need. And when you determine the supplements, you can then find the proper amount, so the supplement is truly effective and not harmful. Supplements can cause adverse reactions or simply be a waste of your time and money. It's ideal to divide supplements up into 2–3 feedings a day, so that they can aid your animal's body in a more balanced and efficient manner.

Probiotics—When I worked with a holistic vet, she said that probiotics are one of the best daily supplements there are. Our dogs, cats and horses are on daily probiotics. Consider feeding this supplement daily and not just when an animal is sick. Probiotics help put good bacteria in the gut, which can help the immune system to function properly. Animals especially with ear, skin and digestive conditions can benefit. Look for a pure probiotic that does not have dairy (lactose, whey), sugars, grains, fillers or "extra" stuff, which most do. Dairy products can actually cause stomach irritation, including yogurt, cheese, and even goat's milk. Keep in mind that many dogs and cats don't do well on dairy.

Digestive Enzymes—You might think this is redundant, but if your animal has stomach issues and is on a good probiotic, they may also need a daily digestive enzyme to help their body process the food. My 6-year-old adopted, former sled dog, Jackson, needs both a probiotic and digestive enzyme right now, as does Allison's senior dog, Bob.

Joint Supplements—There are many on the market and getting the right one and the right amount is important. Methylsulfonylmethane (MSM) is the one we most frequently use to help animals. They may need from 250 mg–20,000 mg daily, depending on their mobility condition. It's often best to avoid combination products, as they normally have very little MSM in them. My senior horses get MSM. Allison's senior dog receives it and just needed an increase.

Often joint supplements are needed for the rest of an animal's life, and the amounts may increase over time. Bandit was my 8-year-old, 40-pound dog that would get up from a nap and drag his back legs. His core diet was good, but he needed a joint supplement. He started taking 10,000 mg of MSM daily and stopped dragging his legs. As he got older, his dosage needed to increase to 20,000 mg daily, but his mobility remained great, and he lived until 16.

Glucosamine sulfate and glucosamine hydrochloride (HCL) can also be beneficial. We've seen 100 mg to 5,000 mg used with animals.

CBD oil can work magic. It certainly has helped my senior horses! They get 15–20 drops each twice a day of 500 mg potency in a 1 oz. bottle. My senior dogs get 4–6 drops each twice a day. It has helped Lady greatly with her focus and has improved Moose's mobility.

Omega 3s—Salmon, krill, or green lipped mussel oil can be fantastic. If your animal has cancer, flaxseed oil may end up being better for them, as sometimes fish oil can negatively affect the growth of cancer cells. Phytoplankton is a non-fish oil, omega 3 product that may be beneficial. The amounts and needed duration can fluctuate.

Herbs—If animals were able to, they'd eat the herbs they need in the wild. Herbs come in various forms: tinctures (liquid), powders, capsules, fresh and dry. Milk thistle can be super for cleansing the liver and liver issues, especially in the springtime. Marshmallow can do wonders for urinary problems. Spirulina, blue-green algae and kelp have helped many with skin and respiratory conditions.

We think herbs are wonderful, but there are precautions to consider. For instance, Chinese herbs are great but can cause stomach irritation, because they are so strong. Herb amounts are crucial and normally given for only a specific amount of time. There are numerous herbs that can benefit your animals, but please consult a professional before giving any herbs to your animals.

So, in conclusion, the right food is not only healing but also about prevention. You need to look at the whole diet and be an ingredient detective by examining labels closely. Keep in mind that diets need to be adjusted throughout the lives of your animals, depending on the seasons and their health. You can use muscle testing to determine the ideal diet, including proper amounts and duration of supplements. You can discuss your animal's diet with your holistic vet or wellness coach.

ACTION: *While there may be multiple changes you need to make to your animal's diet, write down at least one nutrition change that you can make now that you think will benefit your animal.*

Energy Elixir

Just like the animals draw on energy from the natural world around them and have the ability to utilize the energy for healing and other purposes, so do you. We all have this innate energy inside of us. You can use this energy to help heal people, animals, nature and Mother Earth. Energy work may be considered the quintessential elixir of life. You are working with energy that will never harm you, a person or an animal. There are some forms of energy work that require a special attunement or training. Basic energy work does not. And the animals want to make sure you are aware of this.

Energy work can help heal an animal, person or a situation. If there are emotional issues due to a traumatic situation, such as abuse, neglect, or trauma, energy work can help release and heal those emotions. For behavioral conditions such as nervousness or hyperactivity, energy work can help reduce stress and anxiety. If an animal or person is sick or injured, energy work has the ability to speed up the healing. If there is a serious illness, energy work can help bring comfort and be a great complement to conventional treatment. If a person or animal is facing surgery, energy work given prior to surgery can lessen the amount of anesthesia needed and help the post-op recovery go more quickly and smoothly. If an animal or person is ready to pass on, energy work can help bring peace and comfort to both of you during this difficult time. It really seems to help them relax so they are at peace and ready to move on.

Energy work helps you to experience freedom from fear, judgement, and love without conditions. You can become more grounded and in tune with yourself, people, animals, nature and Mother Earth. Keep in mind that you can send energy by distance to an animal, person, place or situation by setting your intention. You can even use a stuffed animal or doll to represent the animal or person. You can send healing to the past or future, which is especially helpful if the condition is a result of emotional issues of any kind.

Energy work can be offered to a person or any type of animal. The techniques discussed here will focus on animals. Since animals are more sensitive, guidance is helpful. You can use these same methods on a person, though. Start off the session by letting the animal know that they should only take the amount of energy that they want. Make it your intention to offer healing energy for their greater good. You can call on animals, nature and Mother Earth to guide you. This can be done silently. Sit on the ground, chair or couch 5'–10' from the animal. Gently tap on your collarbone and thymus with your fingertips to activate your energy. The thymus is located in the center of your chest, where your heart chakra is located. A chakra is an energy center in the body, and there are seven main chakras. Then rub your hands together to activate the yin and yang.

Energy is given to animals by your intention and you allowing the energy to flow through your hands. You may start out with your palms directed toward the animal and see what response you get from them. If an animal moves away from you, stay where you are. It's possible the energy is too strong for them. The animal may move away several times to a distance they feel comfortable at to receive the energy. If they move into another room or across the pasture, that is an indication that they do not really want the energy work at that time or are through with the session. Energy should not be forced on an animal.

During the session, some animals will brush against, lick, or smell your hands. Animals will stand, sit, or lay down. Some will even reposition their bodies. During a session, you may notice the animal chew, lick, sigh, yawn, drool, pant, close their eyes, fall asleep, stretch out, twitch their muscles, quiver, make vocalizations, etc. In time, after several sessions, the animal will probably allow you to get closer to them. In fact, some animals will come to you and place their body where they want you to offer energy to, such as their head or hindquarters.

Keep in mind that you never need to touch an animal with your hands, unless you are guided to and they are receptive to it. Let the animal guide you on how much energy they want. They may just want a minute or may want 30 minutes or more. If you are offering energy because an animal is sick or injured, shorter, more frequent sessions are preferred to longer, less often ones. You can benefit your own well-being if you offer yourself just five minutes of daily energy work.

When you can get closer to the animal's body, you can offer different energy options. For overall wellness, you can sweep their energy field, also called an aura. Set your intention that you are clearing their energy field. Place your hands an inch above your animal's body. Then move your hands from their head to their tail or down out their feet. While you move your hands, you will move your fingers as if you are playing the piano in slow motion or creating gentle rain drops. When you get to the end of the tail or feet, flick your fingertips with the intention that you are getting rid of any negative energy, and envision it dissolving.

If there is an area of illness or discomfort, set your intention that you are pulling the pain or illness out, and make a grabbing motion with your hand towards the area of concern. After you make the grabbing motion, shake your hand towards the ground, and intend that what you pulled out is disintegrating. Do this process several times or until the animal moves away, which indicates they've had enough.

Remember, you do not ever need to touch the animal's body when you are doing energy work on them, unless you feel the desire to do so, and they are receptive to it. Keep in mind that animals are more sensitive than we are, and many would prefer that your hands aren't placed on them during this time. After an energy work session, an animal may pant, yawn, sneeze, cough, have discharge, be thirsty, dizzy, tired, or have excessive urination/defecation due to the energy/blockages being released from their body. Make sure water is available for both you and the animal.

My energy work training began with Reiki, which you may be familiar with. I learned and taught a newer energy, considered from the same source as Reiki, called Shamballa or Multidimensional Transformation energy work. My partner and I have studied other forms of energy healing over the years, and we were guided by the animals to develop their own style of energy work. As energy work is central to our practice and teachings, we have been blessed with guidance from the animals to create Sacred Animal Spirit Alchemy™ (SASA). While this is a specific form of energy work that you might be interested to learn, just remember that you can offer basic energy work as outlined above.

Marlie was a rescued, yellow lab (pictured here), that had been used as a puppy-mill breeder. While vets had healed her physically, she was deeply, emotionally scarred. She would stay in her crate and not engage with Cindy's other lab. We tuned in to Marlie and found out that she never got a chance to be a mom and worried about her puppies and future. Allison and I did energy work on her. We told her it was okay to let the past trauma go and that she had a forever home with Cindy. As Marlie lay on the floor, her body shook with tremors. She let out the longest and loudest moan. We had never seen or heard anything like this before. Her horrible past was released. She then got up off of the floor, bounced around and wagged her tail for the first time ever! Marlie was like a puppy again, wanting to engage with people and animals. She was forever changed!

ACTION: *Consider offering basic energy work to your animals, yourself and others. Write down those you feel could benefit from this. You may want to keep a journal of your sessions to track details such as methods offered, duration and results.*

Flower Power

There's a good chance you are familiar with Rescue Remedy. For those of you who are not, Dr. Edward Bach, a London medical doctor, created Bach Flower Remedies in the 1930s, the first flower and tree essences. His Rescue Remedy is made from five of the 38 essences and is most beneficial in traumatic situations.

Essences are created by placing a flower or part of a plant or tree in water. It is then placed in sunlight, which allows the water to take on the vibrational energies of that part of the plant or tree. Dr. Bach believed that diseases result from imbalances or negativity on the soul level. He studied the link between emotional states of his patients and disease and realized that flowers and trees had healing properties. Even though these essences were originally created for people, animals are very sensitive, so the effects can be very healing. A growing number of pet parents, holistic animal practitioners, and rescue groups have found out how wonderful the essences really are.

Flower essences work on a vibrational level with the ability to affect people and animals physically, mentally, emotionally, and spiritually. They help bring the body back in balance and are gentle. We are not aware of any side effects. If you select the wrong essence(s), nothing should happen. Remember that essences work on an emotional or energetic level. If you can help your pet become an emotionally balanced and happy animal, then it's possible that any behavioral problems will be greatly reduced or eliminated. And if the health issue is due to an emotional imbalance, the essences can diminish or resolve the issue. This also applies to humans.

While a single flower essence is more effective because it's more focused, most animals need a custom remedy made of 3–7 essences in order to properly hone in on their issues. Muscle testing is the key to finding the right flower essences for an animal or a person. (We'll discuss this method in the next chapter.) While there are many flower and tree essences on the market, we have found that the Bach ones work very gently on animals.

To create a custom blend, take two drops of each remedy selected, place them in a 30 ml bottle, and fill the bottle with purified, spring or filtered water. The bottle will last for approximately 4–6 weeks and should be stored in the refrigerator. Shake the bottle before offering. Essences work based on frequency, not the number of drops given. A person or animal takes 2–4 drops several times a day. If you offer more drops, you are simply wasting it. Ideally, the drops are best placed in your animal's mouth. If that's not possible, you can put the drops on a small piece of food to ensure they ingest them. Make sure you do not let the dropper touch anything, so that you don't possibly contaminate it. If your animal is too weak, you can place the essences on your hands and rub them onto your animal's ears or pads of their feet. On hoofed animals, an ear is a better option than the hoof.

In our experience, improvement can be seen within the first few days when a custom blend is given. If you speculate to determine the remedies, or use a generic combination blend on the market that was created to help *some* cases with a specific issue, a longer time frame will more likely be needed to see results, if any.

Keep in mind that there are things that may have happened to your animal before you got them, even if they came into your life at six weeks of age. Even if you were present for their birth, what you have seen in their life doesn't take into account any past lives they have had that could affect their situation. Something may have even happened to them in the womb. So, you see, basing remedies off of your own knowledge may not hold the key to providing the most help for your animal.

Please note that a new situation, which affects your animal's behavior in a negative way, especially if they had been doing well, may not respond to the current blend of essences. Situational changes may require new blends.

While some of the essences may remain the same, most likely some different essences will be needed to help the animal through this new situation. Custom flower essence blends are beneficial, as they are personalized based on what is going on at that moment in an animal's life. And truthfully, having a custom blend applies to you, too. Often, we have found that when an animal needs a custom blend, the pet parent may need one, too. And yes, frequently it is the same blend as the animal's.

Saucey, the spicy little calico cat we mentioned in the previous chapter, came to live with Allison after her owner passed away from cancer. She had never been around dogs, so you can imagine her horror to be thrown in a house with not one, but two, 40 pound dogs! Saucey found a safe haven, much to their dismay, under the table between the sofa and chair, where no one could get to her. She only came out to go to the litter box, which all of a sudden was very often— poor little thing had diarrhea. Well, most people would pull out the standard diarrhea medicine to stop it, take their cat to the vet or worse, perhaps get rid of them.

However, in this case, the diarrhea was undoubtedly brought on by her emotional stress and baggage from losing the only life she had ever known and being thrown into a scary, new world. The perfect thing to get to the bottom of the issue (pardon the pun) and release Saucey's emotions was a custom, Bach flower essence blend. We muscle tested for a custom blend and after taking it for about 3–4 days, not only was her diarrhea gone, but she was no longer hiding under the table. Saucey had made friends with the big dogs and was finally at home. The essences worked so well because they are gentle, and they get to the root of what's going on, rather than stopping the symptoms temporarily.

ACTION: *Write down if you feel your animals, yourself or family members have emotional issues or health conditions as a result of buried or suppressed emotions. Consider how flower essences may help.*

Amazing Aromatherapy

Aromatherapy can be important to your animal's body, mind, and spirit. Essential oils are extracted from the flowers, leaves, bark, roots, stems, seeds, or fruit of a plant. The oils are then either inhaled from the bottle or a diffuser or diluted with a carrier oil and rubbed into the skin. The use of aromatherapy dates back to Egypt, over 5,000 years ago. Documented veterinary remedies date back to the 18th century. Human massage practitioners may let you inhale essential oils, or they may apply a blend of oils directly to your body. Some equine and canine massage practitioners offer this option for animals. An increasing number of pet parents enjoy the benefits of aromatherapy, when used safely.

Essential oils can be considered antiseptic, antimicrobial, detoxifying, and rejuvenating. They can help your animal with emotional issues such as anxiety, nervousness, stress, and those that are hormone related. Physical issues such as skin problems, joint conditions, digestive problems, respiratory conditions and circulatory problems may benefit from essential oils.

Aromatherapy can affect your animal on various levels. The essential oil or hydrosol (a by-product of oils so considered a safer option by some) is inhaled by your animal or applied to their skin. When your animal's nose senses the oil, the molecules of the oil send a message to their brain where memories and emotions are stored. Because of this, your animal's body releases chemicals, such as serotonin, which can have a calming effect, noradrenalin, which can stimulate and rejuvenate, and endorphins, which can help to relieve pain. After the molecules are processed by the brain, they enter the bloodstream and make their way throughout your animal's body. If the oils are rubbed in with a carrier oil or applied with a spray bottle, the molecules are absorbed through the skin and enter the bloodstream that way.

When I lived in Texas, flies and mosquitoes were a nightmare for my family for much of the year. I constantly created essential oil blends to use on my human and animal family. While a spray bottle worked well, I also made a salve to apply to the belly line and legs of my older horses to keep the flies away. I muscle tested to determine the best oils each time I made blends, which included oils such as cedarwood, citronella, clary sage, eucalyptus, geranium, lavender, lemongrass, and litsea.

Lavender can be very calming and is probably the most popular essential oil used for both people and animals. We created a blend we like to call *Mellow Fellow*. It can help anxiety and fear at home, on travels, or at shows. If thunderstorms or July 4th fireworks upset your pet, it may help provide relief. In a four ounce, spray bottle, put two drops each of lavender, sweet marjoram, roman chamomile, and sweet orange essential oils, and then fill it with purified water. Shake the bottle before each use. This blend has even stopped two cats from fighting in the kitchen during mealtime when a pet parent sprayed the blend into the air.

It's not recommended to use essential oils on birds and small animals, because their bodies may be unable to handle them and cause them to become sick or possibly die. Use caution with small dogs and cats. Many people feel oils should not be used with cats because they believe a cat's body is unable to properly excrete the oils through the liver. There is even concern that the inhalation of oils can harm cats, so if you allow your cat to just smell the oil, make sure you don't force them to. Some people say they have used oils successfully on their cats without any harm. If you choose to go this route, proceed with caution.

Even dogs and horses can be very sensitive to essential oils, whether used topically or in the air. Topically, animals can have skin reactions, hair loss, seizures, or worse. While diffusing oils may smell good in your home, your animals may not be able to tolerate it, even if you think they can move elsewhere in your home. Just because oils are good for you does not mean they are good for any of your animals. A woman diffused oils in her home and found her dog dead the next morning. This made the Houston news. Horrors like this do happen, even with therapeutic grade oils and good intentions. Just most pet parents don't hear about the dangers of oils, because so many people have jumped on the oil bandwagon. This has led to growing numbers of misuse of oils in various applications among pet parents and even professionals. There is a reason that the Pet Poison Helpline website has information on the dangers of using oils for both cats and dogs. Animals are brought to the emergency room all the time, and some of them don't make it.

There is a time and place for oils. With precautions, they may be just what your animal needs. We have used oils for many years. You can select some essential oils or hydrosols that you think would be beneficial for your animal based on their physical, mental, or emotional condition. Most companies that sell aromatherapy products will have general information regarding the effects of a particular oil or hydrosol. When you try aromatherapy with your animal, the safest way to offer it is to open the bottle and let them smell it if they choose. If they do not seem interested or turn their head away, you could try another kind. If your animal is receptive, they may lick, chew, snort, curl their lip, try to follow the bottle, or even put their mouth on it. Muscle testing is the best way to determine if aromatherapy should be used in the first place and if so, which oils, the application method, the number of drops of each oil, the frequency to offer, and the duration. With precautions, essential oils may be very helpful to your animal's well-being.

ACTION: *Write down if you think your animal or you would benefit from any essential oils.*

Humble Homeopathy

I first learned about homeopathy from the holistic vet I used to work with. She used homeopathy as one of her primary methods to help animals. She recommended the book, *Homeopathy Beyond Flat Earth Medicine*, by Timothy R. Dooley. After seeing her in action and reading about the basics in the book, I bought my first homeopathic kit from her.

Homeopathy is a healing system developed by Samuel Hahnemann over 200 years ago and based on the thought, "like treats like." This form of vibrational medicine addresses the emotional and mental reasons behind an illness. It has been said that Gandhi felt homeopathy cured more cases than any other method, along with being cost effective and non-violent.

Some people believe that physical illness is the physical manifestation of an illness or imbalance in the emotional or mental bodies of a person or animal. Homeopathy has been used on humans for many years and has become more recognized as an alternative treatment for animals. Some holistic veterinarians and pet parents use homeopathic remedies because they can help heal their animals of many mental, emotional, and physical health problems. We recommend everyone have a homeopathic kit in their house, which contains the most commonly used remedies. We even travel with our 100-remedy kit on vacation, as you never know when it will come in handy. A 50-remedy kit is a more affordable option and contains the top remedies you will most likely use.

Homeopathy is based on the premise that any substance that can produce a certain set of symptoms in a healthy person or animal will cure those same symptoms in a sick person or animal. The difference between pharmaceutical drugs and homeopathic remedies is that the drugs treat the symptoms and homeopathy treats the *cause* of the symptoms. Homeopathy is becoming more popular, because many people are aware of the possible side effects of drugs and how taking them can weaken the immune system of a person or an animal.

Homeopathic remedies are created by taking an infinitesimal amount of the natural substances, diluting it (called *potentization*), and then shaking it (called *succussion*). This process is done by machine. As odd as this may sound, the more a remedy is diluted (called *potency*), the stronger it is. Homeopathic remedies are available in tiny pellets and liquid form. The potencies we will discuss here are the ones that you can purchase without a prescription.

Most people prefer to use a "30C" potency because "X" potencies tend to require the dose to be repeated and/or it takes longer to see results. If the symptoms worsen before they clear up, this is called aggravation. Some people prefer the "X" remedies because it's unlikely they'll cause aggravation. However, aggravation normally happens when you have chosen the right remedy and healing is occurring. When using a "30C" potency, aggravation may not occur at all and if it does, it probably won't last longer than an hour. Homeopathic veterinarians may use a stronger potency of homeopathic remedy, which they may only give the animal once, and then it's recommended to wait a week or more to see results.

Homeopathic remedies may be a little more challenging to administer because of the precision of the technique, however, it can also be easier to work with these tiny pellets or drops as opposed to pills, capsules, or powders used for non-homeopathic methods. It is best if you only use one remedy at a time, so that you can tell if that remedy has worked.

Place the pellets or drops in your animal's mouth. You need to make sure that you don't touch the pellets or drops with your hands or that may neutralize them. You can put the pellets or drops onto a spoon to get them into your animal's mouth. If that's too difficult, you can let your animal lick the pellets out of a dish or dissolve the pellets in a small amount of water and pour it (or the drops) on a small food item that will absorb it, like a small piece of bread. If possible, you won't feed them anything for at least 30 minutes prior to or after you've offered the homeopathy. You should offer the remedy to your animal and observe. Homeopathy is amazing, and sometimes you can see results within a few hours.

Some companies that sell homeopathic remedies will include guidelines, such as they may recommend you give a dose every 3 hours for up to 4 doses, lengthening the intervals between the doses when it appears to be working. However, we highly recommend using muscle testing to determine if homeopathy will help the situation and if so, then determine the proper remedy, potency, frequency, and duration.

Some popular homeopathic remedies, along with common issues for animals are listed below. You may look into homeopathy for acute conditions. Chronic conditions are best helped by homeopathic professionals.

- **Aconite (Monkshood):** shock, fear, sudden onset, eye pain
- **Apis (Honeybee venom):** stings, hives, allergic reactions, itching
- **Arnica (Leopard's bane):** trauma, shock, bruises, soreness, sprains
- **Arsenicum (Arsenic):** food poisoning, diarrhea, vomiting, anxiety, fever, abandonment
- **Cantharis (Spanish fly):** urinary tract problems, burns, abscesses
- **Euphrasia (Eyebright):** eye wound/pain, conjunctivitis, watery eyes
- **Hypericum (St. John's wort):** nerve injury, mashed toes or tail, punctures, burns
- **Ignatia (St. Ignatius bean):** grief, anger, neurotic behavior, starvation
- **Ledum (Marsh tea; wild rosemary):** punctures, bruises, stings, dislocations, stiff, swelling

- **Nux vomica (Poison nut):** vomiting, constipation, over-eating, motion sickness, gas
- **Phosphorus (Phosphorus):** pre-and post-sedation, bleeding, poisoning
- **Thuja (Arbor vitae):** post vaccination, infection, warts

Tracie adopted Paris from the pound. The vet diagnosed this sick, little dog with distemper and possibly parvo. While Tracie was doing what the vet prescribed along with daily energy work, Paris got weaker. Using muscle testing, Paris' diet was adjusted, and she was started on the homeopathic remedy, Thuja. This remedy can help to battle infections. The homeopathy helped Paris to make a full recovery along with energy work and the right diet.

ACTION: *Write down if you think your animal or you may benefit from homeopathy.*

Color Therapy

Color therapy is also known as *chromatherapy* and originated in China, India, and Egypt. Light is a form of energy, since it has its own vibration. Humans have three kinds of cone in their eyes, which react to different wavelengths. Dogs, cats and horses have two kinds of cones. Even though animals can't see all of the same colors that we do, it is the energy or vibrational frequency of the color, not the color itself, that aids in healing. Color affects every living being, whether they see it or not. Since every living being is made of energy and every color has its own energy, colors can be used to restore balance.

We feel every animal has a healing color that can assist them on a physical, emotional or spiritual level, or whenever they are facing any kind of challenge. Color therapy can simply be offered by placing a towel, sheet, or blanket near the area your animal spends a lot of time. You can also get different colored bedding materials or accessories like bowls, collars, halters, brushes, etc. You can even frame construction paper so that your animal doesn't tear it up, if that's a concern. You can find that ideal color for your animal by muscle testing.

Light blue can be great for calming and general anxiety. It can be beneficial for shock and trauma, so keep a light blue towel or blanket handy in your home and vehicle, in case of emergencies. Light pink may help separation anxiety. Yellow can be beneficial for grief and depression, as it brings joy. Greens can be wonderful for grounding and focus. Red can help increase appetite and confidence. Because this color aggravates, it shouldn't be used on animals with aggression or health problems, as it can make their condition worse. And orange has properties similar to red, so use this color with caution.

Simone was a lovely Siamese/tabby mix cat that was taken in by a wonderful no-kill shelter after being forgotten in the local animal control kill room for a week. To put it mildly, she was terrified. The shelter staff had Simone in a wire crate and a red welding glove sat on top of it, because they couldn't even put food in her cage without her trying to attack them. They did not realize the color red was making Simone more fearful and aggressive. We muscle tested for Simone's best color, and it was yellow. The only thing the staff had that was yellow was a banana, so it was placed on top of Simone's crate. The shelter director said that after the first day, Simone was not lunging at them but didn't want to come out of her cage. On day three, Simone came out and walked around. In a week, she decided she wanted to be on the director's desk and spent the next several months as her desk kitty. Yes, color can be a powerful healing tool, even a banana!

ACTION: *Write down what color you think your animals or you could benefit from right now.*

Charming Crystals

The use of crystals dates back to at least 25,000 BC. The *Ebers Paprus* (1600 BC) states medicinal uses, such as ruby for liver problems and lapis lazuli for eye conditions. Information on the physical and medicinal properties of crystals was written by the Greek, Theophrastus (372–287 BC). The Egyptians and medieval Europeans wore amulets fashioned with crystals and gemstones for their powerful qualities. Today, even the medicine men or shamans of the American Natives, Aborigines, and Bushmen still use stones and crystals. Over 100 years ago, the Curie brothers of France discovered piezoelectricity. Scientists have realized that crystals emit a certain energy vibration.

When a piece of quartz crystal is electrically charged (think of a battery with positive and negative charges) as a result of being compressed, this allows an electrical current to pass through it. A piece of quartz oscillates at a specific rate. This is how they are used in watches. It regulates the energy from the battery and when the quartz oscillates, the gears indicate that a second has passed. The piece of quartz crystal in the watch is measured for its energy frequency and cut to the necessary size. Because natural quartz can have imperfections that make it unusable for certain technical applications, it has been reproduced in labs for use in electronics and even military devices.

All crystals have healing properties that can help people and animals. Crystals and stones can help heal the body, mind and spirit. Here are some examples of common conditions and specific crystals that may help them:

- **Arthritis:** amber (fossilized tree sap), calcite and malachite
- **Digestive Issues:** fluorite, moonstone and sodalite
- **Kidney Problems:** bloodstone, hematite and jade
- **Respiratory Conditions:** amber, labradorite and malachite

- **Teeth Issues:** fluorite, howlite and pink zebra jasper
- **Adoption, Abuse or Neglect:** aventurine, coral and rose quartz
- **Anger or Aggression:** howlite, kyanite and unakite
- **Grief or Depression:** carnelian, pink zebra jasper and rose quartz
- **Fear or Anxiety:** amethyst, aventurine and smoky quartz
- **Focus or Training Issues:** citrine, fluorite and tiger's eye

Crystals can be offered to animals in a variety of ways. They can be placed near the animal or under their bed, making sure they are not stepped on or ingested. Some people use crystal wands to help heal injuries or remove illness and discomfort. Crystals can be placed or held on the animal's body at specific locations such as the hindquarters or back. You can offer your animal a massage with a specially shaped crystal designed for use in a massage. Crystal pendulums can be used to check the chakras in an animal's body to see if they are in balance. If an animal is out of balance, some people use crystals to bring them back into balance. Our favorite way to offer crystal therapy (as seen in the photo) is to place crystal beads in specially made pouches that are worn on the collar or halter.

When animals are receptive to crystals, you will see positive signs such as drooling, licking, chewing, eyes softening, sighing, head lowering, or improvement in their health. While crystals can be helpful, not every kind will have the same effect on every animal. The best way to determine which crystals can help your animal is through muscle testing. If crystal therapy tests strong for your animal, then you can muscle test to determine which crystals will help, along with the best way to offer them.

Some animals may need the crystals for a long period of time, especially if they are ill. For other animals, if the crystals are left on or near them constantly, the energy from the crystals may make them uncomfortable. Some animals are very sensitive to crystal energy, so if you use crystals that are too strong for your animal, use too many crystals, or leave them on or near them too long, you can possibly see a negative reaction. If you have placed the crystals under their bed and they do not want to sleep there, this can be a sign that the energy is too strong for them. If you use a crystal wand on your animal or try to put a crystal pouch on them and they run away, this can be an indication that they don't wish to have the crystals at that time. If your animal wears the pouch and exhibits any unusual behavior, try removing it to see if their behavior returns to normal.

By using muscle testing, not only will you be able to select the appropriate crystals for your animal, you will also be able to determine how long they should be used, thus helping to avoid any unnecessary discomfort to your animal. Keep in mind crystals need cleansing before and after they are used, as they absorb both positive and negative energy from people, animals and the environment. Easy cleansing methods are to use the power of your intention, put them in full moonlight overnight or sunlight for a day, or smudge them with sage.

Sabrina was a dog Janice adopted without knowing any of her past history, like most rescued animals. Sabrina had many social problems: she wasn't properly socialized with dogs or people and lunged and barked angrily at other dogs, etc. We muscle tested and crystal therapy showed up as a method to help Sabrina. Six different crystal beads were muscle tested to go into the collar pouch for two weeks.

When Janice first put the pouch on Sabrina, she came home from work and her dog seemed more relaxed and calm. Janice's mother, unaware of what was going on, even called her to say that Sabrina seemed different. During hikes, Sabrina used to get excited around other dogs but now, she calmed down more quickly. Even when she went on walks in the neighborhood, people commented about how much better Sabrina had gotten. Between the power of the crystals, Janice talking to Sabrina and socializing her, great strides were made.

ACTION: *Write down if you think your animals or you could benefit from crystal healing.*

The animals want you to utilize what Mother Earth has to offer. Think about what ways you've observed your animal draw on nature through their actions. What about you? What have you offered your animals from nature? What have you offered yourself? Think carefully about what you could do now for your animals and yourself. Consider teaming up with a holistic vet or animal wellness coach to help you on your journey.

Chapter 5

The Soul Watchers'
Power of Touch

Never underestimate the power of a gentle touch.
For when that touch is accompanied with pure love
from a kind soul, the heart can be truly affected
to the depths of the soul. When we touch
with our soul, touch knows no physical boundaries
and is only limited by our mind's beliefs.

—GRACE, MY TURKEY IN SPIRIT

Touch can be quite powerful. In this chapter, we will explore some basic touch techniques. Energy work is addressed in the previous chapter and not included here. Based on our experience, most animals prefer not to be touched when energy is being offered, because they are so sensitive.

Mesmerizing Muscle Testing

Yes, this is the part where I explain the muscle testing I've been talking about. When you need to know what's the very best nutrition for your animal, the ideal methods to help them, what products to use, plus other elements in their lives, you can do your best to guesstimate. Or, as John Diamond, MD explains in his book, *Your Body Doesn't Lie*, muscle testing will show you the truth.

Muscle testing is also called applied kinesiology, body wisdom, and energy testing. This method uses the energy of the animal or person's body as a source of knowledge. It is used by holistic veterinarians, animal wellness coaches, naturopathic doctors, chiropractors, acupuncturists, and other professionals. A growing number of pet parents are learning this skill. Muscle testing, used properly, can show you the ideal diet for each animal, including the best foods, supplements, and proper amounts. Keep in mind that if you don't have the right nutrition for your animal, anything else you do will be a temporary fix. We have found that even most animals on holistic diets need their nutrition adjusted at regular intervals, whether it be the core diet, supplements, or both.

Muscle testing also shows you what holistic methods are best for your animal and their order of importance, along with the precise details of any modality. For instance, with aromatherapy, muscle testing will show you what essential oils should be used, the appropriate method of application, and the correct number of drops, frequency and duration. Unsure about topical products? You muscle test. This skill saves you time, money and your animal's well-being.

You can muscle test with a partner or on your own, but muscle testing with a partner is generally easier to learn. (Pictured is my daughter holding Valentine, our chinchilla, and a piece of broccoli.) Muscle testing utilizes your finger

or deltoid muscles (in the top of the shoulder) to provide results. It's not about pressing on an animal's muscles. For instance, if you wanted to check to see what proteins your animal should eat, you would ask out loud, "Should (name of your animal) eat (name of a protein like beef, chicken or turkey)?" If you use the finger method, your partner would then try to pull apart your thumb and middle finger that are held tightly together. With the deltoid muscle, you would hold your arm out to the side, as if it were a solid board, and your partner would try to push your arm down by pressing on your wrist area. If your fingers slide or come apart, or your arm goes down, even slightly, this would indicate that protein is not "good" for your animal at this time in their life. If your fingers remain firmly together or your arm holds strong, then that protein is something they should eat. No matter how hard you try, when the food or product is not ideal for the animal or person you are testing, you can't keep your fingers intact or hold your arm up. It's amazing how this works!

Energy runs through our bodies, and this technique is energy based, so the actual food or product you want to test does not need to be present during muscle testing. You can use an image of the food or product, or the exact name of it. For the same reason based in quantum mechanics, as mentioned in the previous chapter, the actual animal or person being tested doesn't need to be present. There is an energetic connection between all life. You can use a photo or picture the animal or person clearly in your mind.

Muscle testing can be done in the comfort of your home. You can also do this technique in a pet food store, health food store, grocery store, or any other place you shop. You can even browse a catalog or the internet for items you are interested in purchasing and muscle test to your heart's content.

Muscle testing is not about physical strength or willpower, but for the highest good. My husband was interested in purchasing more affordable dog food that I considered "low" quality. I told him that if he could keep his fingers together during muscle testing, we would get this food. He placed his left hand on the bag of food and held his right thumb and middle finger together. He asked out loud, "Is this food a 'good' food for Lady?"

Please note that normally you would use the word "ideal," "best" or "right" instead of "good," but I knew the food was inadequate, so I simply went for "good." At 6'1" and 200 pounds, my husband tried his best to keep his fingers together, which would indicate "yes" this food is good for Lady. But when I pulled on his fingers, they flew apart. I jokingly like to say, we refer to that as a "hell no" answer. No, this food was not good for Lady, and the muscle testing clearly showed that. My husband laughed, as he knew we weren't getting that food despite his efforts to save some money. Ultimately, he knew this would cost both Lady and us, probably in medical bills, in the long run.

While muscle testing is easy to learn, it's best learned in person, through videos or an instructional ebook with photos. We have taught many people to muscle test over the years, including holistic vets. My daughter learned muscle testing when she was twelve years old. My husband muscle tests with me. Most of the time, I do muscle testing by myself. It's a skill you can use for life that the whole family can learn for the benefit of everyone.

ACTION: *Write down the questions you would like to ask that muscle testing could answer, and ways it could benefit your animals and you.*

Awesome Acupressure

While some animals and pet parents aren't fond of acupuncture, which is a method that applies tiny needles to specific acupressure points, simple acupressure uses the gentle touch of the fingers. Like acupuncture, acupressure is part of Traditional Chinese Medicine (TCM) and treats the whole animal as a living being, rather than simply treating the symptoms. Not only can acupressure be done by anyone, anywhere and anytime, there are absolutely no additional tools needed. It can assist in healing health conditions, including injuries, arthritis, skin conditions, digestive disorders and behavioral issues, such as fear, anxiety, aggression or grief.

There are acupressure certifications that anyone can get without having to be a veterinarian, but even if you aren't a certified acupressure practitioner, you can utilize common acupressure points on your animals. Do not fear if you aren't exactly right on the point. This is an energy-based modality, and the energy will find its way to the point energetically, and the animal will receive some benefit. Keep in mind that every animal reacts differently, but for many conditions, acupressure can be very helpful, and most animals will have a good to excellent response to this therapy.

However, there are some guidelines to do acupressure to ensure the utmost care of each animal:

- *Never* use too much pressure. A light touch is all that is needed.

- Do not do more than 6–8 points per session.

- Don't hold each point longer than the animal wants. The animal will always tell you when each point is done, as they will move away, pick up their foot, sit down, etc. Listen to the animal.

- Always do both sides of the body when there is a correlating point, to keep the body balanced.

- Do one side at a time so you only do one acupressure point at any given time.

Some common points that help animals are:

- The happy point to relieve emotional stress—Bai Hui
- The aspirin point for general pain—BL 60
- The trauma point to help bring animals out of shock—GV 26
- The icing point to help bring animals out of a seizure—GV 14

You can do an internet search for these points, and you will find diagrams that show their locations. Muscle testing can show you if acupressure will be beneficial for your animal and help you to determine the best points.

Did you know that the face collar for dogs is based on calming acupressure points? The holistic vet I worked with used a face collar with her dog clients and saw amazing results.

Allison even used a face collar with her dog, Petey, to help him chill out while on a walk. When she got him, he had been a street dog, so had a different experience on how to act around people and other dogs. She started off and placed the face collar on Petey in the house when she was home. She did not attach a leash to it. That way, he could get acclimated to wearing it in familiar surroundings.

The face collar is lightweight but can take dogs a bit to get accustomed to wearing. After about a week, Petey wore the collar as if it were a part of him. Allison started clipping the leash to it in the house to practice with him. Petey did great and in no time, she was able to take him out for walks. This face collar had a wonderful effect that gave him a sense of security and peace, even in new situations, like instant chamomile. Eventually, Petey was able to transition to a regular collar for their walks.

Did you know that the body wrap is also based on acupressure points? Wrapping is a way to help an animal feel calm and safe from their fears. While it doesn't work for every animal, it does work for many. You can wrap your animal with an elastic style bandage. There are also various shirts and vests on the market, even for cats. You can look on the internet for wrap techniques along with how to create your own body wrap or shirt for your animal.

ACTION: *Write down if you think acupressure could benefit your animals and you.*

Emotional Freedom Technique (EFT)

Emotional Freedom Technique was originally created to assist the psychotherapy profession and is commonly referred to as tapping. For many people, it has greatly reduced the therapy time to just minutes or hours. Over time, EFT practitioners noticed that amazing physical benefits occurred: from simple health issues, such as headaches, that vanished, to more serious issues, like cancer symptoms, that diminished. They found the reason this happened was that although, Western medicine doesn't really address energy disruptions in the body or emotional causes, EFT does. Just as in people, animals can have emotional problems that are expressed through health issues or disruptive behaviors, especially those animals that have been through a traumatic experience.

EFT is done by tapping on specific points on the animal that correlate with specific emotions and organs. Surrogates can also be used. Some adults and children use stuffed animals and dolls as the surrogate. You can be the surrogate for your animal. The tap is light with just one or two fingers.

Often, we have found that the pet parent has somehow supported, allowed, or attracted their animal's negative behavior or situation, whether they realize it or not. For instance, if there are two animals that tend to fight with one another, it's possible the pet parents argue with each other. Yes, it's possible for your emotions to affect your animal's well-being.

Muscle testing helps you to know if EFT will help your animal, and if so, which application method is best for the animal. Most of the time, we find that the pet parent should tap on themselves to help their animal, instead of tapping on their animal directly or a surrogate. Most animals prefer not to be tapped on, and the pet parent often needs the benefits as much as the animal does.

During the tapping session, affirmations are repeated to help release the emotional blockages. Set up and reminder phrases are used. The person that taps will speak for the animal out loud or in their mind, and speak as the animal would. For instance, if someone adopted a dog that had an abusive past and is afraid of strangers, possible set up phrases could be:

"Even though I'm afraid of people,
when they come to our home, I am okay."

"Even though I'm afraid of people during our walks,
I love and accept myself."

"Even though I'm afraid other people may try
to hurt me, I trust my mom/dad."

Reminder phrases take key words or concepts from the set up phrases, such as "fear of people in my home," "fear of people on walks" or "fear of people harming me."

Allison shares the touching story of her dog:

Petey was our adopted street dog that we had worked very hard to rehab using crystals, energy work and positive training. He had come such a long way, and he was the best dog UNTIL... all of a sudden, he started to lunge and bite people (luckily most were family, but we lost a few plumbers and electricians) that had entered our home, BUT not when they entered-only when they headed for the door to leave our house. Very odd, right?

Well, we had been burglarized just before the "leaving, lunging and biting" began, and this really affected my husband—he felt so betrayed with such a sense of loss. After I exhausted all my HAC modalities and holistic tool kit, we tried EFT. During the EFT tapping session when we had connected to Petey, it was revealed that he was mortified and felt like a failure because he had slept right through the burglary—and had never barked or alerted us! Petey saw how sad it made "daddy," and he vowed never to let anyone ever again leave our house and take stuff that meant something to us.

Wow, all of this behavior was out of love and loyalty! We did a few rounds of tapping, reassuring Petey that he's a good dog and to let go of feeling less than, and we assured him that anyone we allow into our home can leave with anything we give them. Just one session of EFT was all that was needed. Several dinner parties and many years later, Petey can meet, greet and say goodbye to everyone that visits! We haven't had an issue since that one EFT session. It's amazing how quickly it can work and release so much, even decades of emotional pain, trauma or blockage.

Often, one session of EFT is all it takes to get results. Depending on the situation, you may need to do daily sessions with your animal for several days or a week before you achieve the desired outcome. Some people find these results so hard to believe that even when there is improvement, they shift into worrying if it was enough, or if it really worked. If you start to stress over the situation, the issue can return because your animal may tune in to your emotions. A remedy for this is to use the EFT on yourself to help with your emotions.

EFT has been done successfully by distance with animals and people. Since it is energy based, distance is not a factor. For instance, an EFT practitioner living in the U.S. was able to help two cats in South Africa become more confident and less depressed due to the traumatic experience of getting declawed. More professionals and pet parents have become aware of EFT and utilize it to help heal physical, mental, and emotional issues. Anyone can learn how to do this simple technique, including children. You can look for a local class or find instruction on the internet.

ACTION: *Write down if you think your animals or you could benefit from EFT.*

Magical Massage

Many people enjoy massage, and your animals are no different. Massage is a touch technique used to maintain and improve physical and mental health. It can help prevent injuries and aid the body with healing. Massage causes yours and your pet's body to release endorphins, which are the natural chemical that relieves pain and makes you both feel good. It can also strengthen the bond between you and your animal. If your animal acts injured or ill, you should consult with a vet for a proper diagnosis to make sure massage is appropriate.

Massage increases circulation and helps eliminate toxins and wastes. It can improve the condition of your animal's skin, coat, gums, and teeth. Massage can improve joint flexibility and muscle tone, which is especially beneficial to older animals and those with active lives such as performance animals. This method can help their attitude and ability to focus, which affects behavior, training, and competitive performance. It's very popular with sport horses and dogs that compete in agility and flyball. During massage, some people will even use aromatherapy or a crystal massage wand (as seen in the photo) to enhance the benefits.

Massage can help animals with behavioral problems when you gain their trust through the act of touching. It can calm down a nervous or hyper animal, help a shy or submissive pet feel more secure and relax an aggressive or dominant pet. Massage can help animals recover from injuries or chronic conditions. It can reduce the recovery time from soft tissue injuries. This technique can provide relief from muscle soreness and spasms, and relieve pain and discomfort associated with conditions such as arthritis and hip dysplasia.

Pepper was a 12-year-old schnauzer that had been limping for over three weeks due to a strained ligament. It was difficult for him to stand up or walk. Pepper's pet parents learned some massage and basic energy work techniques from me. (An ideal combination!) His movement improved, and he was able to run around the home again.

You can perform a wellness massage on your animal with a simple technique that uses light touch with your fingertips. Do this weekly or monthly to notice changes in your animal's body. Look and feel for heat, swelling, sores, discharge, odor, tenderness, etc. Have your pet checked by a vet for any areas of concern. You can do this massage in any order that you and your animal prefer:

- Touch your animal's head with the fingertips of both hands, and run them down their cheeks to under their mouth.
- Check their teeth and gums without blocking their nose.
- Feel and look into their ears.
- From their ears, move your hands down their neck to their throat.
- From their throat, move your hands down their chest, shoulders, and front legs. Flex their legs and check their paws, pads, or hooves.
- From their feet, move your hands down their stomach, sides and back.
- Next, check their back legs the same as you did their front legs.
- Check their rear area including genitalia and tail. Doing this last, allows the animal to move away when you get "personal."

ACTION: *Write down how massage may benefit your animals or you.*

Touch is powerful and can be utilized in so many ways. Perhaps you currently use touch in some form, such as petting or brushing. Think about how you can incorporate the power of touch for your animals and yourself.

Chapter 6

The Soul Watchers' Heart and Soul Connection with You

Become pure again. We will help you if you listen.
This is the path to surrender and to peace.

—HOPE, MY WHITE DOVE IN SPIRIT

The Heart and Soul Connection

If you have looked into "New Age" thinking at all, you have probably heard this phrase, but what really is a heart and soul connection? The heart is considered the source of life, both emotionally and physically. The soul is referred to as the spiritual component. The *heart and soul connection* is the beautiful link between yourself and an animal, nature or person that unites you together on a mental, emotional, physical and spiritual level. This connection can be thought of as heart to heart, mind to mind, soul to soul.

The more you become open to possibilities and are willing to step outside of your box, the more you become connected with all there is. Whether or not you know how to communicate with animals on a telepathic level, the more deeply connected you are to animals and nature, the more you will find yourself able to be in tune with all of life.

The animals know what you are capable of. They want the best for you. And that starts with you wanting the best for yourself.

ACTION: *Reflect upon what the heart and soul connection truly means to you. Write down how this concept makes you feel.*

Grateful Gratitude

While this title may seem redundant, we should be grateful that we can express gratitude to the animals, and that the animals demonstrate gratitude for us. Be grateful for the incredible animals that are in your life now, those that have shared the past with you, and those that will be a part of your future. Be appreciative for the vast array of nature's bountiful benefits that are provided for you every day. In today's hectic pace, it's so easy to forget to be thankful for all we have in our lives, including the little things.

Thank the animals and nature for their presence, for being there for you. Tell your animals out loud that you love them and are grateful they are in your life. You can even be specific and tell them what they bring to your life such as love, joy, happiness, laughter, companionship, comfort, and protection.

Talk to nature. Tell the flower how beautiful it is. Let your energy and words flow to them. Hug the tree, and let it know how magnificent it is. Let the creek know you appreciate the precious water that flows forth. Mother Earth provides us with necessary nourishment for our bodies. Thank the food and drink you consume. Be grateful for the clothing you wear, the roof over your head, etc.

When you live from a *heart and soul* place, it's easier to live in a state of gratitude for everything around you, for all there is. My daughter told me this years ago when she was a teen. "Mom, every night before you go to bed, say out loud three things you are grateful for that day." I have always thought this was so wonderful and a great reminder that we should be grateful for and acknowledge the many blessings in our lives. I try to make it a daily habit to say, "I am so blessed." There are so many little things I'm grateful for that are present in my life now, and I'm grateful for what's to come in the future.

Have gratitude in your heart, as if your desires have already been fulfilled. The animals and nature are honored to offer so much to us. We should honor them by showing respect and appreciation. It's amazing how verbally expressing gratitude can work wonders in your life.

ACTION: *Write down what you are grateful for in your life and how you can express this to the animals and nature.*

Create Sacred Space

The first step is to look at your environment for yourself and your animals. Sacred space means that you create a natural and energetically clean space, as much as possible. You've probably heard of the expression, "Your body is your temple." What you put on or in your body contributes to the energy in your space. This space affects all that lives there, including your animals. It's also important to remove toxins from your home and yard.

Many products contain harmful chemicals that can have serious consequences such as:

Household products, including cleaners, fresheners, deodorizers, plug ins, detergents, cleansers, dryer sheets, and even soap. I try to avoid ingredients such as Ammonia, Bisphenol A (BPA), Chlorine, Formaldehyde, Phthalates, Perchloroethylene (PERC), Perfluorinated chemicals (PFCs), Per or polyfluoroalkyl (PFAs), Quarternary Ammonium Compounds (QUATS), Sodium Hydroxide, Triclosan and 2-Butoxyethanol.

Lawn and garden products, like fertilizers, weed killers, herbicides and pesticides. I do my best to stay away from pest and lawn chemicals like 2, 4-D, Atrazine, Carbofuran, Coumaphos, Cyothioate, Diazinon, Fampfhur, Fention, Metaldehyde, Methomyl, Organotins, Phosmet and Tetrachloryinphos.

Remove toxins you use on yourself and your animals, such as those in make-up, shampoos, ointments, bedding, litter, toys, and flea and tick control. I try not to use products that contain ingredients such as Benzoate, Blue 1, Cocamidopropyl Betane, Cocamide Diethanolamine (DEA), Dimethicone, DMDM Hydantoin, FC&C Color Pigments, Fragrance, Imidazolidinyl Urea, Methylisothiazolinone, Parabens, Perfluorochemicals (PFCs), Phthalates, Polybrominated Diphenyl Ethers (PBDEs), Propylene/Polyethylene/ Butylene Glycol, Pyrethrins, Pyrethroids, Red 33, Sodium Lauryl/ Laureth Sulfate, Sodium Momoethanolamine (MEA), Sodium Xylene Sulfonate, Tetrasodium EDTA and Triethanolamine (TEA.)

Only get vaccines that are absolutely necessary, and consider getting titers when possible. (A titer test is a laboratory blood test that can show if the vaccines are still effective in your animal's body.)

Look at ingredients carefully on the labels of all products. Just because something says "natural" doesn't mean it's chemical free or won't harm. If the products you use contain chemicals, consider natural alternatives. You can even make your own pet-safe products for your home and animals.

Negative energy is another concern. This energy can affect people and animals on a cellular level. Reduce encounters with electromagnetic fields (EMFs) as much as possible. Unplug and turn off equipment when not in use, if you can. Watch where you put beds and bowls, so that you and your animals do not sleep or eat near high frequencies, like your TV, cell phone or Wi-Fi. Even pay attention to where you are outdoors, such as when you walk your dog or ride your bike or horse. Is there strong energy coming from something such as a cell tower or an electrical substation? Try to avoid such routes. If you live near an area of high energy, there are still things you can do.

Consider placing Himalayan salt or selenite lamps in your home to allow positive energy to flow into your environment. I have multiple lamps in my home, as I also use my home for teaching. You can place a pair of black tourmaline and citrine in the four corners of your home or work space on the lower level to help absorb the negative energy and emit positive energy. Make sure animals don't ingest.

You can cleanse yourself and home with traditional Native American smudging. For those who are not familiar with this term, it is burning sacred herbs or resins. I use white sage and try to smudge at least annually and certainly, whenever I feel it's needed. Light the sage, and let it smolder around your entire body, including the soles of your feet. To cleanse the space inside and outside of your home, let it smolder into every room, including closets and bathrooms. Walk around your home perimeter with the sage. You can even say a prayer about your intentions for the smudging.

Remember, what you put on or expose yourself and your animals to affects, at minimum, the immune system. The more positive energy you can create in your environment, the more in tune with animals and nature you can become, and they can become with you.

ACTION: *Take control of what you put on or near yourself and your animals, in and around your home. Make a list of changes you can make. Start to take action.*

Glorious Grounding

Grounding refers to being present in the moment on a body, mind and spirit level. It's more than just feeling like your feet are underneath you. When you aren't grounded, you may have a hard time focusing and may even feel "spacey." Being ungrounded can cause you to feel tired and make you more prone to illness. Being grounded is an important part of being connected and tuned in.

There are many ways to become grounded, such as the examples here:

- Envision you are a tree, and there are roots coming from the soles of your feet that reach deep into the heart of Mother Earth.

- Picture magnets on the bottom of your feet, strongly connected to a giant magnet at Earth's core.

- Simply stand barefoot on the grass, sit or lay on the ground, or hug a tree and connect to the energy that flows through it.

- Water can be grounding. You can stand in the rain, a creek, or let the waves at a beach gently flow over your feet in the sand. Yes, you can soak in the tub or take a shower, but nature's water can be more effective.

- You may want to hold or wear crystals to help you ground, such as clear quartz, bloodstone, or hematite.

- Some animals are helpful with grounding. You can stand next to a horse and place your hands on them. When you sit on their back, you connect your root chakra (the energy center located in your seat area) to their heart chakra (located at their withers area, beneath your seat). You may be familiar with the incredible impact that horses make in the role of equine assisted therapy. Dogs may try to help you ground and lay at or sit on your feet. Other species may try to assist you, too.

- Tap gently with your fingertips on your collarbone and thymus (located in the center of your chest). This can raise your energetic vibration and help you to ground.

- Speak your intention out loud by saying "I am grounded, centered and balanced." Yes, you can ground with your intention.

- Some people like to meditate to ground. This is discussed in the next section.

The best goal is to feel grounded daily. Even five minutes a day of a focused routine, in whatever way works for you, can help you to become more grounded and make a real difference. If you aren't sure what the best way to ground is for you, then experiment. You can use muscle testing to help you determine your ideal way. You can also go into nature with your animal and have a grounding experience together.

ACTION: *Explore grounding and write down what way or ways work best for you. Aim to ground daily.*

Mindful Meditation

Meditation is useful for more than grounding. Mindful meditation is about meditating with a purpose, even if that goal is just being open to receive whatever happens.

When I teach animal communication classes, I walk students through the process of how to take five deep breaths in preparation for each meditative exercise. It can help to take off your shoes and let your feet touch the ground. Here is what I say in the class:

- Close your eyes.
- Breathe in through your nose and out through your mouth. Allow the breaths to go deep into your body, then slowly release them.
- Breathe in through your nose and out through your mouth. Gradually, relax deeper and deeper.
- Breathe in through your nose and out through your mouth. You are taking slow, deep breaths.
- Breathe in through your nose and out through your mouth. You are relaxing.
- Breathe in through your nose and out through your mouth. You are very relaxed.

When you combine meditation with animals and nature, you can create a deeper and more powerful heart and soul connection with all life. Some people prefer to meditate in silence. Others prefer meditative music. You can meditate indoors or outdoors.

Indoors, I suggest you find a special place where you feel comfortable and where others won't interrupt you. I enjoy soaking in the tub at the end of the day, getting my water just right, and then meditating, even if for five minutes. Sometimes my dog, Jackson, will lay on my bath mat during this time. Calcite, coral, and fluorite are crystals that may help you with meditation and visualization. While you can hold the crystals in your hand during meditation, I've even placed them in and around my tub. Sometimes, I meditate with nature sounds or flute music playing.

Outdoors, nature can provide incredible sounds that can take you on a journey. I walk to the nearby creek almost daily (as seen here). One day, I sat on a rock by the creek's edge and listened. I asked for a message. A stalk behind me gently thumped my back, and it certainly got my attention. *Listen.* I was shocked at what I heard. At first, it was the loud water rushing by with the excess from the mountain's snowmelt. Then I heard it. All of it. It was a symphony. I heard musical instruments and a lady's voice singing, "Ahhhhh." It was lovely. In my mind, I could see rainbow colors and prisms of light that accompanied the symphony.

I had no idea any of this was even possible. I should not have been surprised by what nature has to offer us—and the ability to receive if we just listen. The creek told me that we have to listen quietly. We don't realize what we are missing sometimes. We need to think of the animals that live in the creek and use it. We need to go beyond just what we "see" right in front of us in our lives.

If you can be still and listen, you will hear the messages you need to hear. You will feel what you need to feel. Guidance can come from all kinds of things in nature. Just give yourself a chance and believe you can do this.

The sun then shone a beaming ray of light. It was clearly trying to get my attention. The creek said we need to soak in the rays, and to think of everything that surrounds the water, the life source. We need to soak it in. It is all connected. We are all connected. We need to be willing to get our feet wet, cross that log, walk on the stones.

Nature will support you as needed. You just have to take that first step. Once you do it, keep taking more steps. Nature is there for you.

ACTION: *Try to meditate for five minutes daily. Experiment meditating indoors and outdoors. Journal about what you receive.*

Heart to Heart

The heart has been mentioned throughout this book because it is so important. It goes beyond the amazing love we have for animals. Speak from your heart. Open your heart to all of the possibilities. If you want to connect more deeply to your animals and be open to their wisdom, connect your heart to their heart, which can help to establish a strong heart and soul connection. You can do this in your home or out in nature, wherever you and your animals are comfortable.

Connect your heart to your animal's heart simply by stating your intention to do so, either silently or out loud. Your animal can be in front of you, in another location, or even in spirit. You can use a photo if you prefer. While connecting your heart to their heart is as simple as that, you may want to take it a step further. You may want to picture your heart chakra (located where your thymus is, in the center of your chest) connected with your animal's heart chakra (located at three places: the center of their chest, at their withers, and girth line). You can select one location of their heart chakra and focus on that.

If you desire, you can visualize a more tangible connection between your hearts, such as some form of light or fabric. You may even want to envision this in the color of your choice. For example, you may want to visualize a beam of radiant, lavender light or an elegant, silver ribbon that connects your heart to your animal's heart. This connection process can be simple or more elaborate, as it's totally up to whatever you feel within your heart.

You can set your intention that you are always connected heart to heart with your animals. It's especially helpful to do this process if you wish to tell your animal something, or you want to receive a message from them. If that's the case, ground and meditate, then connect to your animal. If you want to tell them something, then do so at this point. Then be open to receive whatever happens. If you want to receive a message from them, let them know the specifics of what you want, and then be ready for their response. It's a great idea to have a journal with you so that you can record your experience.

ACTION: *For a deeper link, connect your heart to your animal's heart. Write about what connection process works best for you. If you connect with a variety of animals, as each animal is unique, it's possible you will be drawn to connect in a different way with each animal, dependent on what you feel with that particular one.*

Soulful Speaking

While we touched on this in a previous chapter, let's dive deep into how to really "soulful speak." Speak to your animals from your heart and soul. Really, speak out loud to them. Do you know this is one of the top things in life that animals wish people would do more of? Animals want more than small talk. They want to hear how your day was. They want to hear your hopes and dreams. They even want to know when you're worried. Animals want to fully share their souls with you through unconditional love and have you bare your soul in return. When you speak to your animal, you can even envision them inside of a green bubble. Green is the color associated with the heart chakra. If you desire, you can visualize yourself in the bubble with your animal, or choose another color that resonates with you.

Did you know that you can actually learn to understand what animals are saying? While you don't need to "hear" them in return in order to speak from your soul, please know this is your birthright. Everyone is capable of learning to communicate with animals on a telepathic level. It's just a matter of waking up this innate ability. This means you may hear your animal's words, sense their emotions such as love or fear, feel physical sensations such as itching or discomfort, see their thoughts in the form of images, or just know on a deep heart and soul level what they want to share with you. I can tell you that this is truly magical and life changing when you can connect on this profound level.

While this process of "hearing" animals usually takes a one-day class to learn and feel confident, there is an exercise that you can do to help you become more connected on a heart and soul level.

As a first step, spend time in nature. Sit still, listen to the sounds, and feel the sensations surrounding you. Become one with nature. Then follow these steps:

- Set your intention in your mind to find a piece of nature to connect with.

- Now, go look for this piece of nature that calls to you. It may be a rock, stick, feather, etc. When you come across this item, you'll know because it will "feel" right.

- Sit down with your item in nature, or return indoors to your favorite chair, bed, etc.

- Hold your item in your hands, close your eyes, and meditate.

- Ask the item to speak to you and share with you whatever it wants to. You can say this out loud or in your mind.

- Be ready and open to receive whatever you get. You might get images, words, emotions, sensations, or things that just "pop" into your mind.

- Write down whatever you receive. Know that whatever you get, you got for a reason, regardless of how odd it may seem.

- Thank the piece of nature for sharing with you. You may return the piece to nature or keep it to speak to it at another time.

Just speaking out loud to animals can make quite the impact. Tito was a dedicated student of ours who cared very much about animals on a heart and soul level. He worked at a large, dog-boarding facility and knew how talking out loud to the dogs could benefit both animals and people. Tito asked the staff to start greeting the dogs and talk to them every morning. He'd remind the employees, "Talk to the dogs." While they were hesitant at first, as many didn't really understand the benefit, they did so and were astonished when they quickly started to see an improvement in the dogs' behavior, from excessive barking and frenzies to acting calm and attentive. Tito never doubted the results the dogs and staff would experience, as this is the powerful simplicity of the heart and soul effect.

Never underestimate the power of the spoken word, for it is truly priceless. When you speak to your animals, you raise their energetic vibration, and your own. You will not only look at animals and nature differently, you'll see the whole world in a new light.

ACTION: *Write down what you can share out loud with your animals and incorporate that into your daily routine.*

Nurturing Nature

Technology has disrupted lives on various levels, and animals would like us to get back to the "old-fashioned" ways: get back to nature, get out in nature, use nature. Take time to smell the flowers. You can become your own cell tower, connected energetically to the animals and their natural surroundings. Nature nurtures us, and we should nurture nature. The animals want you to embrace it whole-heartedly, on a body, mind and soul level. If you be-

come more aware of nature, you'll realize just how much nature is aware of you.

Seek nature to prevent illness. Call on it to help heal. Nature influences and impacts our whole energy field before it manifests in our bodies. Remember how much nature can help you and your animals by utilizing Mother Earth's medicine chest. Whether you spend quality time in the outdoors, take flower essences, or use crystals for healing, nature is a valuable resource you can't live without. We like to say that now is the time for a double D.A.W.N.:

"Your **D**ivine **A**wareness of the **W**isdom and **N**urturing from **D**omestic **A**nimals, **W**ildlife and **N**ature."

When you are aware of the profound knowledge that animals and nature have to offer and allow them to nurture you, your life will never be the same again. In return, to help all of life, we need to be aware of the actions that we can take and know we can soar to new heights.

ACTION: *Write about any new ideas you have to let nature nurture you and your animals. Write about how you can nurture nature in return.*

Grow Your Garden

Growing up, I frequently watched Mr. Rogers. I loved how he spoke about growing ideas in the garden of your mind. The animals plant seeds in our thoughts and wait for a world-wide harvest. When we can respect and honor all of life, we are flourishing winners in the garden of life. Through this process, we strengthen that heart and soul connection. When you find this kind of deep connection with animals, you will be amazed by how much more clarity you have in life. By taking action, they can even help you with your soul purpose. Walking this sacred path with animals helps you to confidently travel down the unseen road to your soul path with such incredible guidance and wisdom.

Remember, when you utilize Mother Earth's medicine chest and learn holistic animal care in order to help animals, you in turn, learn how you can apply these methods to your own life. From the depths of the hearts and souls of the animals to yours, this is what they truly desire for you.

The biggest mistake or regret you may make is if you hold back on gently immersing yourself into this fantastical world. We often like to say, "Make holistic animal care a way of life, not a last resort." Don't wait until you feel desperate for your animal—or yourself. This is not what your animals want for you, for they know the burdens you can place upon your heart. They want you to grow your own garden, and watch it flourish.

ACTION: *What will you plant your heart and soul garden with? Write how you will take action to help your own life.*

You've always had a heart and soul connection with people, animals, and nature, whether or not you've realized it. Even if you are aware, everyone has room for growth. Awaken or reawaken your heart and soul connection. Embark on a journey that ultimately fulfills the vision of the animals. The more you become in tune on a heart and soul level, the more you are in tune with the mission of the animals. Your quest to seek, learn and act, fulfills their quest to awaken humanity.

Chapter 7

The Soul Watchers' Wish for You

*Be the light in the darkness. Be the safe haven
in the storm. Let no one make you doubt
that you are making a difference in the lives
around you. Approach each day as a new chance
to make things right in the world. Surround yourself
with like-minded people and draw strength from one
another. You are a piece of this magnificent puzzle
and have a very important role to play.
The time is NOW.*

—Stripes, my cat in spirit

Animals offer courage, nurturing and wisdom. They want to help you find your grace and move through life with grace. Let the animals help you. Look at all aspects of your life like never before. Let them take you on a sacred journey of the heart and soul to discover and explore things you have never known. Allow the animals to guide you deeper into the abyss of knowledge you already contain inside of you.

Remember, each animal has their purpose in life. Their role impacts your role. The animals will always be there for you, to show you the way, if you let them. I will never forget when I attended a weekend workshop where our class was learning about angels. From the kitchen, then scurrying across the den floor, came a very large cockroach—straight towards me! This was in Texas, where roaches can get very large. The expression on the host's face revealed how mortified she was to see such a creature in her home filled with students. I quickly announced that I was sorry; the roach was meant for me. It wanted to encourage me to be resourceful and resilient through the changes in my life at that time. The cockroach was gently relocated to the outdoors. This experience was a good lesson for everyone there that even the animals you may fear or dislike can have a message for you.

Remember to make this about the animals, not you, so check your ego. What you do for them, you'll get back in return. Together, we all affect reality. What this really means is that we choose our experiences to create our reality. Remember how we learned that thoughts and intent can affect water? We are mostly composed of water and so is the earth. Time is precious. The more time you spend thinking, the more time your thoughts can impact your life and those around you. How you use this time is what really matters. Will you help to create a ripple effect, sea to shining sea?

As guardians of humanity's souls, the animals are entrusting you with their mission. Help them awaken humanity. If we can wake up, we will *be* more, we will *feel* more, we will *do* more. We will wake up and perhaps take a stand against devastation, such as global warming, habitat destruction, pollution, and the extinction of animal species that we, as the human race, continue to displace without true knowledge or a real plan for what's at stake. If we can wake up, we will understand issues into the physical, such as over-medication and over-vaccination, and the misperception of treating only the symptoms, instead of the whole person and animal at the root of the problem.

You can start making a difference in your own life first. Help your animals, yourself, and those you love. I encourage you not to fall into the inaccurate belief, "But I'm just one person." Even a tiny spark can ignite a fuse.

How might you take action? Awareness is always the first step. You can start small: start noticing your pets' behaviors to see what they are trying to tell you, and if you don't have pets, watch for the wild animals around you. How often do you see a bird swoop near you or land on your lawn and think nothing of it? Look online to understand what message they bring.

You might want to become an animal advocate in some way. Many worthwhile organizations have petitions online, the ability to make donations, and volunteer opportunities. I frequently sign domestic and wildlife animal petitions, make donations to causes that pull on my heart strings, and assist with fundraisers for animal-based nonprofits. When I was in my twenties, I volunteered to help rehabilitate stranded dolphins. When I worked for the zoo, I got to conduct field research on the swift fox *(Vulpes velox)* and participate in a nationwide conservation team to preserve their species. Did you know each year volunteers come out to count the butterflies or birds they see? I enjoyed counting and tagging monarchs during my zoo days.

You could start watching any of the many animal programs online or on cable to understand animals better. You might meet and talk to a neighbor's pet or spend time with the animals at your local shelter that are waiting for their forever home. My business partner, Allison, and I, love being able to help troubled and sick animals at shelters and rescue groups. Choose books to read to your children that have animals in them, so you can teach them. If you don't have children at home, consider an afternoon at the library or your local school, reading to children about animals. Some readers even bring their dog with them.

Perhaps you already take action in a variety of ways. Focus on what you can do, what you are willing to do. You may come up with additional ways to acknowledge the animals' support or help others see the importance of animals in our lives. You may decide to simply further your own understanding and appreciation of nature. Please know that animals have their own paths, just like we do. They know you can't be everywhere and help every animal. Sometimes, they come into this life to awaken feelings or bring people to their cause, and sometimes, their life ends tragically. Whether we realize it or not, tragedy can have purpose and move humanity to take action.

I choose to focus on the beauty of my actions and those in and of this world. I choose to help those I can on an individual basis. I choose to see a universe filled with hope. My cup is half full. Yes, I like rainbows, puppies and kittens. *These are a few of my favorite things.* And you may have guessed, *The Sound of Music* is my favorite movie of all time, to the tune that I even have an autographed book by Maria von Trapp.

I honor the animals' mission, as I continue to grow both holistically and spiritually. I will never stop learning and listening. I want to be a voice for the animals. I know the knowledge I gain is tenfold.

While it's all right for animals to be your best friends, they should not be your only friends. Animals know we need human companionship and that humans affect all of life. But choose carefully, for you can't walk this sacred path alone.

The wolf is probably the most misunderstood animal there is. On the one side, it has the most misplaced hate by man, and on the other, it is the most revered by many as a totem animal. The wolf truly is a fine representative of the lessons we can learn in life from an animal. Imagine yourself as a wolf. The strength of the pack is within each wolf. The strength of each wolf is within the whole pack. It's hard for a lone wolf to survive and flourish on its own. You must find your own wolf pack. Find like-minded people that understand animals on this heart and soul level and want to make a difference. Find your truth. Stand in it. Then find others who will stand with you.

When all you can see is darkness, look deeper. Look in it and through it, to see the light, for it is there. The animals present you with an invitation for transformation. Remember, you don't know what you don't know—until you know.

Animals are so much more, beyond what most people realize. Look at the world from their eyes and their souls. If you ever thought your life didn't matter, the animals have always known it has. It doesn't matter what you didn't know in the past. Right now is what counts. Listen to your heart and soul and those of the animals. They will lead you to great places. Remember to believe in yourself, for the animals believe in you.

We can honor and emulate the animals' sacred path. They are our soul watchers. They are here to teach us to be kindred, fellow soul watchers, and to live life from a state of gratitude. What the animals do, they do for humanity and the world. They want us to understand their vision and assist in their mission. We should think of every being as united as one, connected body, mind and spirit—heart and soul. Like an intricately woven spider's web, we are all energetically intertwined in the delicate facets of life.

So, who are the Soul Watchers? *The animals are. You are. I am.* Together, we can change the world and honor the animals' wish for us.

And now you know the truth. So, be your own creator that weaves a pattern of discovery, enlightenment and fulfillment. Extend those fibers to help humanity awaken their inner wisdom, divine light and sacred connection to all.

Embrace, utilize and share the messages and gifts from the animals, nature and Mother Earth. Let them show you the present, help you learn from the past, and propel you to your future.

Learn it, live it, share it.

ACTION: *Reach into the depths of your heart and soul and write about anything you want to express. Know that the animals, nature, and Mother Earth are here for you. Your life matters. You have it within yourself to make a difference.*

Epilogue

Diamond was my first animal I ever had, a magnificent and cuddly collie. I was ten and so excited for my Lassie dreams to come true. He grew from a puppy into an amazing dog. I taught him many behaviors such as sit, speak, bow, prance, fetch, jump and to pull a cart. I loved him with all of my heart, and still do. So, it's fitting for the animal that started this incredible journey for me to be able to share a part of himself with you:

Sometimes we try too hard in life, and the answers are right in front of us. Live, love, laugh. No regrets. For every step you take leads you in the right direction, whether you realize it or not. There are no mistakes in life. Only lessons learned. Only blessings in disguise.

Know that the animal kingdom is here for you, to help guide you on your sacred path. We have always been there for you, though you may have been unaware of the extent of our presence.

Reach out to us. Call on us. Learn from us. Ultimately, animals and humans are all united as one, working towards the same goal—peace and harmony across the universe.

We are all on the same team. No one animal or person is greater than the other, as we are equal partners in life. If everyone can open their eyes to the truth and come full circle, we each will understand the gifts inside us all.

The animals, nature, and Mother Earth treasure you deeply. Please join us to profoundly awaken and enlighten the heart and soul connection between all life. For you, my friend, are a fellow Soul Watcher, and powerful beyond your wildest imagination. Together, we can accomplish miracles.

In Love and Light,
Diamond

Let's Stay in Touch!

Kim Shotola

The Lightfoot Way

Email: thelightfootway@yahoo.com

Visit
www.TheSoulWatchers.com
to download your audio meditation
and action guide for this book.

We offer these holistic animal-care opportunities:

- OVER **250** EDUCATIONAL ARTICLES
  IN OUR E-NEWSLETTER ARCHIVES

- IN-PERSON WORKSHOPS, ONLINE COURSES,
  AND TELECLASSES

- PROFESSIONAL CERTIFICATION PROGRAMS

- IN-PERSON AND DISTANCE CONSULTATIONS

- RESOURCES AND PRODUCTS

Visit
TheLightfootWay.com

Kim with her wise mare Tara on their Montana property

About the Author

Kim Shotola is a holistic animal care instructor, animal wellness coach, and professional animal communicator. She has been featured on TV, radio shows, podcasts and in magazines, and has spoken at in-person and online events.

Kim's holistic animal care journey started 25 years ago when her horse, Tara, had lameness issues, and she found how supplements helped. Since then, she has trained with many instructors in the fields of animal communication, nutrition, muscle testing, energy work, crystal therapy, aromatherapy, massage therapy, and more.

She worked with animals at the Houston Zoo for over 25 years, where she helped manage the care of over 1,000 domestic, wildlife, livestock, and exotic animals in the Children's Zoo, including the amazing bug house. With her knowledge and skills, she helped bring holistic animal care to the zoo to help the whole animal on a body, mind and spirit level.

Kim taught her first, holistic animal care classes at a holistic veterinarian's clinic in 2006, and empowered animal lovers to help all kinds of animals of all ages to live happier, healthier and longer lives. Since then, she has taught hundreds of students from ages 7–82 from all over the world to strengthen their connection, prevent illness and disease, and heal the animals in their care.

In 2017, Kim moved from Texas to Montana to pursue her dream of living and teaching near Yellowstone. She still travels to Texas throughout the year to teach and see her family. Kim and her husband share their home with three dogs, two horses and an albino chinchilla.

For more information about Kim, see THE LIGHTFOOT WAY'S website at: TheLightfootWay.com, under the ABOUT US tab.

Made in the USA
Monee, IL
10 July 2023

38611567R00075